A

HANDMADE

COTTAGE

THE ART OF CRAFTING A HOME

JODIE MAY SEYMOUR

murdoch books
London | Sydney

CONTENTS

INTRODUCTION

Hello reader, and welcome to my handmade cottage. My journey into craft and 'handmade' began many moons ago when my husband and I moved into our first home, a small Victorian cottage. We had little money to furnish the house, so I started looking for the things we needed – tables, chairs, cabinets, curtains – and I quickly discovered it was all going to cost a small fortune. I scoured charity shops, car boot sales, antique shops and reclamation yards, and decided that rather than be put off by craft tutorials I'd just have a go at upcycling, and figure things out for myself. Instruction manuals and complicated measurements are lost on me, as are recipes with long-winded instructions (which might explain why I'm such a bad cook), but just 'having a go' seemed to work well for me when it came to craft and home-making (though still not so much when it comes to cooking).

I taught myself basic sewing skills, collected from nature, and slowly over time I crafted, upcycled and filled our house with ramshackle treasures until I had made the home I always wanted. My passion for all things handmade was born. I started a craft club, became a craft columnist for the local newspaper (alongside my main job as a singer/songwriter and singing teacher) and I began writing a craft blog. Ten years later the result is the book you now hold in your hands.

I think a lot of us would love to have a go at making things but we think it's either too costly or it's simply beyond us. But hopefully with these simple but effective projects you will see it is absolutely achievable, regardless of your skill and ability. I regularly find myself referring back to my own instructions for making things and I thought it would be so lovely to compile a collection of all my favourite projects in just one book.

So put the kettle on, turn the pages and let your mind wander. I'll be there to guide and help you through each of the projects, step by step, as though you were sitting in my craft circle. Hopefully you'll find yourself returning to this book like an old friend, for guidance or inspiration for many years to come.

THE ART OF
CRAFTING A HOME

ANTIQUE SHOPS, FLEA MARKETS,
AND CREATING A HOME
THAT IS QUINTESSENTIALLY YOU

You may be creating a home from scratch or simply looking for new ideas to help you refresh your living spaces. The chapters that follow look at inspiration for every room and include step-by-step projects, but before we start, here is some essential know-how for creating a home that is quintessentially you, as well as top tips for finding those hidden gems that make a house a home.

FIND YOUR INSPIRATION

When it comes to design and style, you need to get an idea of what it is that you like. It might be one style or era or it may be a combination of a few. I didn't really know what my style was initially, but once I started browsing charity and antique shops I found I was drawn to certain things. I quickly fell in love with old rustic furniture, and objects from the Victorian era, with my eye homing in on humbler items from that period – think simple wooden farmhouse furniture, old shutters and cotton lace linens. But I also love my surroundings to be nature-inspired, so I forage and use shells, branches and dried flowers where I can. My husband says he daren't buy anything for me unless it looks like it has been crafted by woodland elves, which is probably a safe bet. That said, I also like some of the retro elements of the 50s, 60s and 70s and the occasional Scandi-style piece appeals to me, so it is a combination of all of the above that makes my house my home.

If you're not sure what you like, try looking to the past and see what it is that brings you joy. You'll soon be drawn to certain objects, styles and eras. You could spend a quiet afternoon in a library or an old bookshop looking at styles through the ages, but seeing things in the flesh and being able to touch them is far preferable, because you'll be more able to 'feel' something that way. While social media is full to the brim of inspiration, it can also be overwhelming, and you can quickly end up following current styles that are trending rather than finding the things that really make your soul sing.

The most beautiful homes are often the most interesting and eclectic ones, and they are that way because the people living there are etched into their surroundings. It's easy to mimic a show home but without pouring love and care into a home it can feel soulless, regardless of how much that rug costs. Our primary goal here is creating a home that we want to live and spend time in.

LOOK BEYOND APPEARANCES. It's amazing what you can do with a lick of paint. When looking for things like furniture don't be put off if it's unfashionably shabby or the wrong colour, as we can have that fixed in no time. I once found an ugly old brown bathroom cabinet at a car boot sale. Painting it white and swapping the tacky white plastic knob for an ornate ceramic one completely transformed it. To buy it like that would have cost a lot of money, so do always look beneath the surface and try to see the bare bones of the furniture.

FABRICS. Whenever you find a fabric you love in a charity shop, buy it. There are endless uses for fabric – tablecloths, cushions, pillows, chairs, coverings, stools, lamps etc – so it is always handy to have a fabric stash. I often check out the long skirts in charity shops – in fact, it was mostly clothes, and skirts in particular, that were repurposed into bunting for our wedding day (see page 255).

NATURE INSPIRATION. You'll find many country cottages are a reflection of the landscape that surrounds them and I just love that. I find it incredibly fulfilling moving in time with the rhythms of the season. I'm immersed in it where I live now, but even when I lived in a busy market town I always took time out to be in nature as it fills me up. I'll often take my basket on walks as I usually end up finding bits to decorate the house – pine cones, fallen branches, lichen-covered twigs, wild berries to make jam or flowers for arrangements (and when I say arrangements, that can simply mean sticking them in a jug or pitcher). You don't need to live in the countryside to do this, as a wander in your local park can be just as fruitful.

YOU CAN DO THIS. When friends or family visit my home, one of the things I'll often hear is 'Oh, isn't that lovely! Where did you find it?'. When I tell them I made it myself they usually reply 'Aren't you clever? I could never do anything like that!' But I didn't study art and design, and I didn't take part in a single craft course. I simply gave it a go and you can too. Basic sewing, for example, is easy – put the thread through the needle, stick in the fabric, go in-out-in-out, and secure with a knot. It's that simple! We just get overwhelmed by unnecessarily complicated instructions and assume it's beyond our capabilities, but it absolutely isn't.

START WITH SOMETHING SIMPLE. A lot of things you already own can be given a new lease of life. Take a good look around your home at the items you already have that might benefit from a makeover – this could be a mirror that needs a lick of paint, a bedside table (nightstand) that could be revamped or perhaps you have some old jam jars that could be transformed into lanterns for alfresco dining. One of my favourite hacks

is to take a very cheap plain cream window blind (shade) and add a lace panel across the bottom of it to give it a soft, feminine, country feel. Little additions can make the biggest transformations.

JOIN OR START A CRAFT GROUP. Even if you have no experience whatsoever, joining a craft club is rewarding and so much fun. Crafty people are often lovely souls and are always ready and willing to share their skills. I learned so much from the ladies in my craft club; they helped me to patchwork, to crochet, to cross stitch and it didn't cost me a penny (except for the large quantities of tea and cake we consumed in the process).

A GUIDE TO THRIFTY SHOPPING

I will happily admit that I cannot pass a charity shop, car boot sale (garage sale), antiques shop or flea market without being lured inside. While some secondhand shops occasionally have a musty smell to them, do not let that stop you. Once you get used to shopping secondhand you will never look back. I regularly save a huge amount of money on furniture, kitchenware and clothes, as well as sourcing gifts from these places too. Shopping this way really is a win-win since we are also helping others by contributing to charities, it's good for the environment as it has little carbon footprint, and since we are recycling goods we can rest easy, knowing we are doing our bit for Mother Earth. That said, I know that entering such places can be a little daunting for some if you're not used to shopping in an Aladdin's cave so let's break it down and you'll be a beady-eyed little magpie in no time.

ANTIQUES SHOPS AND FLEA MARKETS

I find great comfort in spending time in antiques shops and I will often take refuge in one if I'm feeling a little low. I think this is because in this fast-paced ever-changing world, it is a comfort to know that in an antique shop, time is standing still. Everything that surrounds you has outlived the people of its time and it has somehow survived to tell its tale, which gives these items such a special quality. When I wander through these places I feel that many of these objects carry that past with them; you can almost hear the music in the dance halls when you pass the ladies' dancing shoes and shawls, and you can smell the pies fresh from the old ovens when you handle the old original pans and kitchenware. They are stories for the taking and that is why I love them.

PROS

THEY ARE A SHOPPER'S PARADISE. If you love the rustic antique style, you won't have to look hard for beautiful things for your home and garden in these places. Unlike charity shops (where you often have to dig around for the good stuff), in a good antiques shop or market it is all laid out for you. You might still have to sift through a little but I wager that you'll probably walk out laden with goodies.

QUALITY CRAFTSMANSHIP AND INVESTMENT. The saying 'you get what you pay for' really does ring true in this case. The pieces you find in an antiques shop are usually authentic and can be of excellent quality. Take antique furniture for example – in some cases a piece has lasted hundreds of years, so it's more than likely to go the distance in your family home, unlike the cheaply made furniture we find in so many chain shops nowadays, so you know what you are buying is quality craftsmanship. Antiques can retain their value, too. So if you ever decide to sell them, you may be able to sell them for a similar price.

YOU CAN HAGGLE. This depends on the shop of course so it's worth getting to know the ones in your area, but you'll soon establish which ones are reasonable and which ones are overpriced. Some are extremely reasonable and you can buy beautiful pieces for a third of the price on the high street or in the shopping mall. When you do decide you want something, always ask the dealer 'What is your best price?'. They may not budge, but more often than not they will lower the price.

GRAB A BARGAIN AT AUCTION. Checking out your local auction house is especially good if you are looking for larger pieces of furniture (although they can be a good source of smaller items, too). Buying at auction can be thrilling and you really can grab a bargain. However if you have a history of problem gambling or you have no self-restraint when it comes to money, then this probably isn't the best environment for you as you do need to be aware of getting caught up in the fast-paced excitement, which can lead to paying over the odds. If you do fancy giving it a go, then perhaps sit in on

an auction first before you take part so you can see how it all works; that way you won't get carried away or overwhelmed. Some auctions are very easy to take part in, as you simply view the items, jot down your best price (what you'd be willing to pay) and hand it in.

CONS

KNOW YOUR SHOP. Antiques shops really do vary, from the fusty old stores with lovely old rustic housewares that you and I love (and can afford) to the kind that sell the really high end, stately-home, one-of-a-kind objects that I dare not even pick up. You'll soon know it when you walk in and spy a price tag in the thousands – the person behind the counter will raise one questioning eyebrow at you, you'll feel like Julia Roberts in *Pretty Woman* and you'll immediately walk out again. These are often the kind of antique shops that people go to for serious investment purposes. So don't be put off. Just tick it off your list, and go find other more suitable ones in your area.

THE PRICE. Some antiques shops are very expensive. Even if they're not of the calibre mentioned above, some just charge top dollar. Meanwhile, another shop might sell exactly the same things for half the price, so again, don't be put off. Also, don't be afraid to haggle and don't be afraid to query something if you are unsure; I once found a faux enamel soap dish with a hefty price tag that I'd recently seen much cheaper in a high-street shop! It was clearly from there and was being passed off as an antique, so do speak up if you smell a faux rat.

CHARITY SHOPS AND CAR BOOTS

Charity shops and car boot sales are excellent places to source goods. You may also know these places as thrift stores and garage or yard sales. They really are such a big help to those on a small income and for those looking for homeware treasure. However, they can also be overwhelming to many, because unlike a normal shop where everything has its place, in a charity shop, at a car boot everything is in a bit of a jumble so you have to work to find your treasure. But like anything, it just takes a bit of practice and it will all become easier, I promise.

PROS

THE PRICE. You can find everything in these places – furniture for the home and garden, kitchenware, clothes, bedding, cushions, and more – and it's all incredibly cheap. I bought the vast majority of our furniture from charity shops, and often you can grab a super bargain too – by that, I mean the shop doesn't always realise the worth of something they are selling. Things like copper pans and antique lace can be snapped up in these places too, while to buy new or from an antique shop would cost far more.

ORIGINALITY. One of the things I love about charity shopping is wandering around not looking for anything in particular, only to find something so original and unusual that you would never have found (or looked for) it elsewhere. It's these quirky little curiosities that are often the things that can really give a home its character.

CONS

THE ENVIRONMENT. Charity shops can sometimes smell a little musty which some may find off-putting, but it's just the smell of old fabrics. Things can also be a bit disorganized at times as they can become overwhelmed with donations so it can be tiring on the senses scouring the shelves. But do persevere because…

YOU HAVE TO WORK FOR IT. The old saying that one person's trash can be another person's treasure really rings true when it comes to charity shops and, in particular, car boots. Good car boot or garage sales can be busy and you may have to rummage through quite a lot of what you may consider junk before you find the good stuff. So arrive early, eat beforehand as you'll need the energy, stay hydrated, then go forth and forage.

HOW TO BE A MAGPIE

KNOW YOUR SHOP. There are several charity shops in my town and I've got to know their layouts well. Find a couple you can start visiting regularly. If they are located in a busy town they will usually have a high turnover with new items arriving on their shelves all the time, so pop in each time you pass. Shops generally reflect the area they are located in, so if you visit a charity shop in a very well-off area you can expect to find some lovely quality goods and designer clothes, but you should also be prepared to pay a much higher price too. That said, don't assume anything as there is always treasure to be found, even in the most unlikely places.

HOMING IN. The aim is to train your eye so you can spot things quickly and easily, and not spend ages scouring the shelves every time. The next time you're in a charity or antiques shop, try this approach: once you have assessed the layout of the place, take it section by section. I always head straight to household and then comes the crucial bit: homing in. Cast your eye over the whole shelf, then scan it again slowly and just wait for something to jump out at you – it might be an object, a colour or a pattern. If nothing jumps out at you, don't be disheartened; just move on to the next section and try again. Some days I walk out with armfuls of goods, and some days there is nothing. But if your eye is drawn to something, then...

PICK IT UP QUICKLY. The things in these places are one-off items – they don't have more stashed out the back. So I guarantee that as soon as you turn your back, Mrs Miggins from number 92, who has been eyeing that teapot from behind the shelf of jigsaw puzzles, will swoop in the very second you move away and she will buy it. So if you're unsure, just pick it up anyway and walk around with it until you decide.

IF IT BRINGS YOU JOY, BUY IT. Don't worry about where it's going to fit into your home, just buy it. That may sound reckless but I stand by it. Finding objects that spark joy and make you 'feel' something is a precious moment so if you love it, buy it. You'll find the right spot for it and if you don't, then sell it or give it to someone you know will also love it. If you'd like your home to reflect who you are, then don't be afraid to be spontaneous with your buying; it will make it more fun and your home will become more eclectic and original and, ultimately, more you.

THINGS DON'T NEED TO MATCH. This depends on your style of course, but if you're reading this book I'm guessing you also love the eclectic, rustic cottage style. Your home is likely to be far more charming and characterful if things don't match: dining-room chairs, glassware, crockery, cutlery, plates, bowls – simply buy what you're drawn to and the rest will fall into place, and because it's all mismatched, your random purchases will work together in perfect harmony.

WHAT TO WATCH OUT FOR

So you've found something wonderful and are about to hand over your cash. Now is the time to take a final moment to have a good look over it and make a final assessment before buying. Because all of these things are secondhand and they have lived a life before, do bear the following in mind.

FABRIC. Make sure it can be machine washed, hand washed or at least dry cleaned. You don't want your home to smell like an antiques shop, nor do you want to bring dust mites into your home. If it's woollen and is covered with bobbles, that is fine as you can hand wash it and use one of those razor-type gadgets to remove the bobbles and have it looking like new in no time. If it's a fine, delicate piece of lace, a careful hand wash will be fine, or you can simply air it and refresh it. However, if it's a smelly but gorgeous pair of curtains, they will definitely need a good clean, as would a rug, so do check what the item is made from.

WOODEN ITEMS. If it's wood furniture you're buying, look out for active woodworm. Woodworms leave little holes in the wood and many old pieces of furniture have scars of ancient woodworm. That is fine, as this can often add to the character of the piece, as long as it's ancient and not currently active. Active woodworm often leaves frass (droppings) next to the holes, which look like fine sawdust. If a piece does have active woodworm it can be treated with chemicals if you're prepared to do that. If you're not, leave it behind and move on.

LEAD PAINT. Some old painted furniture may have been painted with lead paint. This is fine to touch and use, provided it's not chipped or flaking, as the danger is in consuming paint chips and inhaling the paint dust (so sanding down such furniture would be extremely toxic, even when wearing a face mask). Young children would be particularly at risk if they were to chew on or bite furniture with lead paint. If you're unsure about a piece, you can buy a lead-paint testing kit (make sure it is EPA recognised). If it is lead paint, you can still strip the piece down but you would need to follow specific steps and safety protocols as well as using liquid paint remover instead of sanding. If you want to paint over it, you can do so with an encapsulant, which is a specialist paint that will seal the lead paint. I've tested many items but thankfully they've never been positive for lead.

ELECTRICAL ITEMS. If you've found an old lamp it would be worth getting it looked over by a qualified electrician to make sure it adheres to current safety standards. Shops selling such items are obliged by law to test items themselves but some may slip through the net, especially if you obtain it through a private sale. Do check, and if you are not satisfied, have an electrician give it the once over.

BASIC TECHNIQUES

A BEGINNER'S GUIDE
TO SEWING, DECOUPAGE
AND PAINTING FURNITURE

In this chapter I'll explain the basic techniques used in the projects in this book. You will probably find yourself referring back to this chapter as you work through some of these makes, or you may use it as a simple refresher. Either way, do not feel you need to read this whole chapter in one go. Instead, I suggest you first flick through the book and pick something you would love to make. Then come back here to find the relevant basic instructions and take it one step at a time.

Keep in mind that all projects are for beginners and experienced crafters alike – the level of detail you add to your project is up to you, and the more you craft, the more you'll finesse your skills. So just dive in if you like the look of something, and enjoy where it takes you.

THE ESSENTIALS

I'm not giving a long list of things you might need as you don't necessarily need a lot of specialised equipment to craft. We may be led to believe we need special tools/cutters/gauges but often we already have equipment we can use. For example, while a right-angled ruler is useful, a regular ruler is also absolutely fine. While a cutting gauge is handy for cutting wallpaper, good scissors will also do the job.

Within each of the following sections (and within each project) I have listed the bare essentials that you will need to complete the project, and sometimes there will be some optional things, too. As for the rest, you can build your toolkit over time.

LEARNING FROM OTHERS

Books and videos can be extremely helpful when it comes to learning new skills, but nothing beats human interaction. There were so many things I wanted to learn when I started out so, as well as teaching myself, I founded a craft club, and it was one of the best things I ever did.

SEWING

You really don't need much at all when it comes to sewing. Aside from a sewing machine, which can be very useful, a small basic sewing kit with just a few needles, some thread, fabric scissors, a tin of pins and a pin cushion will have you well on your way. Here is a bit more information regarding sewing essentials.

ESSENTIAL TOOLS

SEWING MACHINE. I highly recommend you treat yourself to a sewing machine if you don't already own one (see buying advice on page 26). If you already own a machine, your essentials are sewing machine needles (which should be changed regularly, and need to be the right needles for the thickness of your fabric) and sewing machine oil, as your sewing machine should be topped up regularly.

GOOD-QUALITY THREADS. Whether sewing by machine or by hand, good-quality thread is essential. If your thread is too thin it will break easily, too thick and it won't be easy to sew with. Your best bet is buying from a reputable brand (I like Gutermann). You'll need matching colours for whatever it is you are working on, but you can build up your colour stash over time.

A SELECTION OF NEEDLES. Buy a small pack of needles in a variety of sizes for hand sewing. For plain cotton fabric use a regular sized needle, but if sewing thick material you'll need a thicker needle, and if sewing something very delicate use a very fine needle to avoid leaving visible holes. You'll soon learn which needles to use for each job.

FABRIC SCISSORS. It is well worth buying a good pair of scissors that you use only for cutting fabric. Store them with your sewing kit and don't ever be tempted to use them for cutting paper or anything else, as this will blunt the blades.

SEWING BY MACHINE

If you like the idea of sewing and making soft furnishings, I highly recommend getting a sewing machine. It makes such light work of sewing and it's so satisfying to use; I love the hum of my machine and how the fabric flies through my hands. It takes such little time to create something unique and the things you do make will stand the test of time.

My sewing machine is a very old vintage Singer machine that belonged to my husband's great-grandmother, who was a seamstress. It is so old it doesn't always sew in a straight line (you can see evidence of this in the last step of the simple cushion project on page 133!) but I still love it. I have two modern machines that can do a lot more, but I just prefer my simple no-frills machine.

BUYING A SEWING MACHINE. If you are new to sewing, my advice is to buy a basic machine. Whether it's new or secondhand, modern or old, don't be tempted to get a fancy machine and risk being overwhelmed by so many different functions. I'd suggest a simple, no-nonsense machine and once you've mastered that, you can always trade it in for a fancier model, though chances are the basic one will probably be all you ever need.

Ideally look for a mechanical machine that has a range of basic stitches, with a foot pedal so you can control the speed. If you want to make cushions from thicker fabric, you'll need a machine that can handle medium/heavyweight fabric too. Always go for a reputable brand such as Brother, Bernina, Pfaff, Janome or Juki (bear in mind Juki and Bernina are more expensive). If you can't afford to buy any of these machines new, perhaps look for a secondhand machine rather than buy a cheap, inferior machine. Some stores sell sewing machines under their own brand, which can be a cheaper option – just make sure you read all the reviews before you buy, to check how experienced sewers have rated the various models.

SEWING MACHINE CARE. When you have your machine, do care for it – the manual supplied with the machine will tell you what to do. Most machines need oiling regularly (I never knew that, and couldn't work out why mine rusted up like the Tin Man). They also need to be thoroughly cleaned from time to time (I wasn't aware of that either, until mine stopped working because it was filled with so much gunk and fluff inside!). If you look after your machine, it will last for years.

GETTING GOING. Once you have your machine, I suggest getting help because if you're an absolute beginner, setting up a machine and learning how to use it can be baffling and frustrating. Initially I was going to include a long list of tedious instructions on how to work a sewing machine, but I feel there is no pleasure to be found in learning this way. Some instructions work fine on the page, but learning to use a sewing machine is much easier in person.

By all means follow the instructions that come with your machine if you want to, and you may find videos for your make and model on YouTube, but if you do struggle, just seek help rather than be put off altogether. Try asking a sewing friend or find a local person who does clothing alterations. Tell them you are a beginner, that you have a new machine and are looking to get a bit of help with it and offer to pay for their time. They may not accept a penny as crafty folk are often very generous with their time and will just be happy to help. Or consider booking yourself on a one-day sewing course. It may initially seem like a lot of money for just a few hours of tuition, but it's all invaluable knowledge and you'll gain a lifelong skill so it certainly pays for itself.

The most basic stitch on a sewing machine is called running stitch, and that is the only sewing-machine stitch I use in this book. The only other thing you need to know is how to finish that stitch. If sewing by hand you make a knot to secure once finished, but on a machine the process is slightly different, although just as simple. When you get to the end of your sewing, hit the reverse button on your machine and reverse sew for a few stitches (this is known as backstitching), then sew forwards again for a few stitches and stop. Lift the needle and foot, and snip your threads. (On a machine, this is also the way to secure the start of your line of stitching.)

SEWING BY HAND

Basic hand sewing is easy. You thread the needle, put it in the fabric and pull it out again, it really is as simple as that. But google it and you wouldn't think so, as there are hundreds of different stitches and technical terms out there. So here are the basic sewing stitches needed for the projects in this book. With these stitches you can join any fabric pieces together and hem any curtain. If you want to know more stitches and techniques, there are plenty of instructional books and videos out there. If you struggle with written instructions (and it's not always easy portraying steps in imagery), do look at videos too as seeing it live may make more sense to you.

THREADING THE NEEDLE. To begin, cut a length of sewing thread and feed the thread through the eye of the needle. When hemming, a single thread is sufficient (you make it too thick by using a double thread, and the hemming more likely to be seen).

STITCH LENGTH. You can vary the length of any of these stitches to suit your project. The rule of thumb is the smaller the stitches, the stronger they will be. Longer stitches might be fine for hemming a curtain, but on a pair of trousers (pants) that will see more action a smaller stitch is preferable as it will have a stronger hold, so adjust according to your item and fabric. You'll soon get a feel for these things and instinctively know what to do.

BASIC HAND-SEWING STITCHES

These stitches are extremely easy to do, so follow the step-by-step photos and it should make sense to you.

KNOTTING THE THREAD. The knot needs to be large enough not to be pulled through the fabric. Thread the needle and pull the thread through until the tail is in between your finger and thumb. Then wind that end around the needle three times and pull off with your fingers, tightening it into a knot as you do.

Alternatively, wind the end around your index finger (for a small knot wind it around once; for a bigger knot wind it several times). Roll the loops off your finger using your thumb which will twist the threads together, then pull the threads together with your fingers to create the knot (see below).

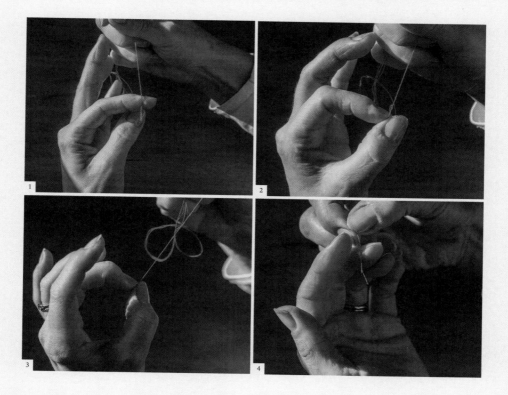

RUNNING STITCH

Running stitch (also known as straight stitch) is the most basic stitch in sewing and embroidery. You work in an up-down motion, pushing the needle up through your fabric, then back down again at small regular intervals.

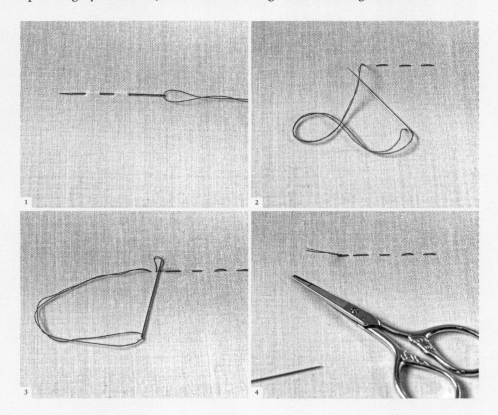

STEPS 1 & 2

Thread the needle and tie a knot in the end of the thread. With the wrong side of the fabric facing up, push the needle down through both pieces of fabric and back up again a short distance away. Continue at regular intervals. You can vary the length of your stitches depending on what you are working on.

STEPS 3 & 4

To finish, knot the thread by making a tiny stitch, but before you pull the thread all the way through, pull it a little way then pass your needle through the loop from front to back once, then twice, then pull taut to make a knot. Leave a little tail of thread of about 2.5 cm (1 inch) and snip.

BACKSTITCH

This is similar to the running stitch but it's a lot stronger, so use it when you really want to reinforce a line of stitching.

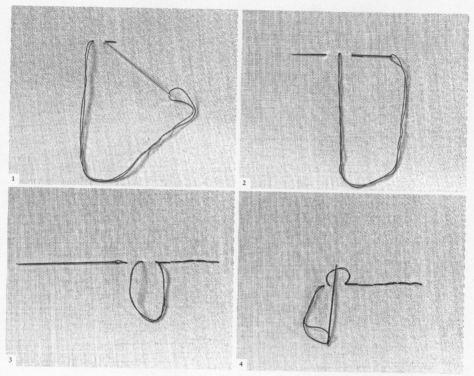

STEP 1

Thread the needle and tie a knot in the end of the thread. Push the needle up through the fabric from the back and insert the needle back down into the fabric, about 5 mm (¼ inch) from the first stitch, like a running stitch. Push up again 5 mm (¼ inch) along, but this time instead of moving forwards another 1 cm (½ inch) as you would in a running stitch, go backwards and push down into the end of the previous stitch.

STEPS 2 & 3

Come up again 5 mm (¼ inch) along from the last visible stitch and repeat.

STEP 4

To finish, knot the thread by making another tiny stitch, but before you pull the thread all the way through, pull it a little way then pass your needle through the loop from front to back once, then twice, then pull taut to make a knot. Leave a little tail and snip.

WHIP STITCH

This little stitch is ideal for hemming and consists of small diagonal stitches. You may find this stitch easier if holding the fabric vertically.

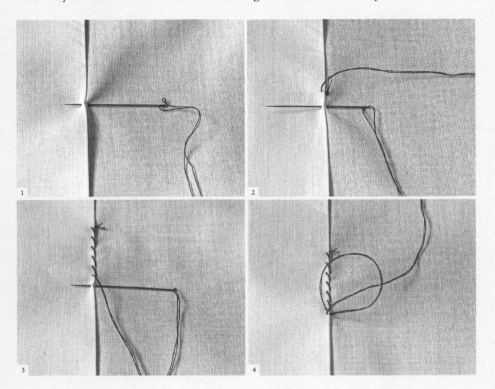

STEP 1

Thread the needle and tie a knot in the end of the thread. Catch a tiny bit of the fabric and a tiny bit of the folded hem and pull the thread through.

STEPS 2 & 3

Repeat this step but 5 mm (¼ inch) along (or however long you want the stitch to be) and continue to the end.

STEP 4

To finish, knot your thread by making another tiny stitch, but before you pull the thread all the way through, pull it a little way then pass your needle through the loop from front to back once, then twice, then pull taut to make a knot. Leave a little tail of about 2.5 cm (1 inch) and snip.

SLIP STITCH

This stitch is ideal for hemming, especially with a double folded hem (which means it has been folded over twice) as most of the stitches will be hidden in the hem allowance.

STEP 1

Thread the needle and tie a knot in the end of the thread. With the wrong side of the fabric facing up, pick up a tiny piece of the fabric below the folded hem with your needle.

STEP 2

Push the needle into the fold directly above, then come out again 5 mm (¼ inch) along, pulling the entire length of the thread through.

STEP 3

Pick up another tiny piece of fabric directly below the fold and repeat.

STEP 4

To finish, knot your thread by making another stitch, but before you pull the thread all the way through, pull it a little way then pass your needle through the loop from front to back once, then twice, then pull taut to make a knot. Leave a little tail and snip.

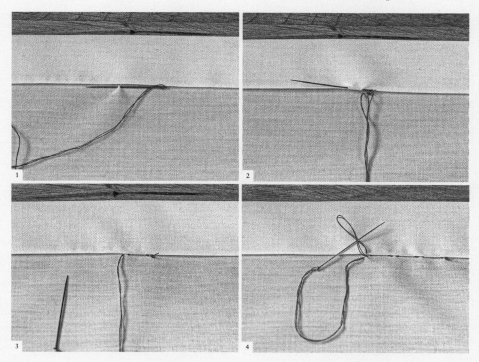

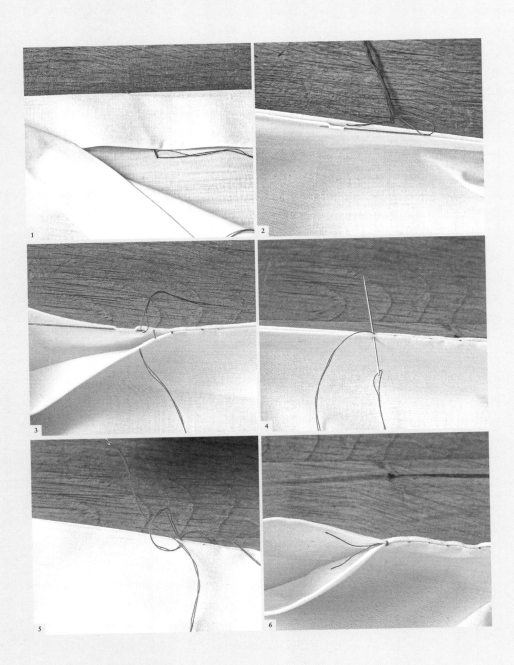

BASIC TECHNIQUES

INVISIBLE STITCH

Also known as ladder stitch or blind stitch, this is a very handy stitch because it is almost invisible. It is very similar to slip stitch (see page 33), except here you make both stitches the same length, moving from side to side to create a 'ladder' that will close together tightly when pulled at the end. It is an ideal stitch for closing gaps in seams, soft toys and cushion covers. Note that it's not the strongest stitch so if you need your item to hold fast (for example a cushion cover) then perhaps use a strong thread to help reinforce. I use this stitch to close up the keyhole cover on page 159.

STEP 1

Thread the needle and tie a knot in the end of the thread. Start by pushing the needle up through the fold on one side and pull the entire length of thread through, securing the knot.

STEP 2

Holding the two folds of fabric together (like a sandwich), take the needle directly across to the other side, pushing it into the opposite fold, take it along (actually, under is more accurate) 5 mm (¼ inch), then come up again, pulling the entire length of the thread through again.

STEP 3

Head back over to the other side and repeat, pulling the thread taut as you go. When you've finished the seam, pull the thread gently one more time to make sure the seam is closed tight all the way along.

STEPS 4, 5 & 6

To finish, knot the thread by taking the needle over the top and back through both edges, but before you pull the thread all the way through, pass the needle through the loop and pull taut to make a knot. Then go over the top once more into the same hole and run it down through the centre (so it's hidden) and snip.

DECOUPAGE

The rather fancy French word decoupage simply means the art of decorating surfaces by applying cutouts of paper, then coating with several layers of lacquer or varnish. It originated in France in the 17th century as a means of decorating furniture with pictures. Decoupage is probably the technique I have used the most around my home because it is so versatile, and can quickly and easily transform anything, anywhere into something unique. I have used it on furniture, walls, food trays, windows, Easter eggs, lampshades, memory boxes... you name it, I have probably decoupaged it.

You can transform a piece of furniture or even an entire wall in your home using decoupage. A children's room is a great place to have fun with it, as you'll see on pages 250–253. Look to books, magazines, wallpaper and napkins for your inspiration and see where it leads. Once you've finally made something I bet you'll find yourself bitten by the decoupage bug, just as I was.

CHOOSING YOUR SURFACE

You can decoupage onto almost any hard surface. Wood works especially well and that is what I mainly use, but you can also use plastic, metal, cardboard, ceramics and glass. If you want to decoupage your item and then sand it down to achieve a distressed faded look, this technique will only work on unpainted porous wood. Regardless of what you use, I'd suggest doing a test patch initially.

Craft superstores sell a vast selection of papier-mâché boxes and model animals that you can decoupage, along with various designs of decoupage papers. However, all you really need is probably already in your home – a small wooden box, terracotta plant pot, old wooden stool or chair, coffee table, empty food can (ideal for storing pens) and more. If you can't find anything suitable, pop along to your local charity shop or car boot (trunk) sale and you'll soon find something that catches your eye.

DECOUPAGE ESSENTIALS

You don't really need much at all for decoupaging. The projects in this book use a few different techniques, and these are the essential things you will need.

- Paper or napkins, in your choice of colours and patterns
- PVA or Mod Podge glue
- Paintbrushes
- Brayer (a hard roller to help remove any bubbles) or plastic ruler, for wallpaper decoupage
- Clear varnish, lacquer or Polyvine Decorator's Acrylic Varnish
- Clingfilm (plastic wrap), for creating distressed, faded finish
- Handheld sander, for creating distressed, faded finish (see page 51)

DECOUPAGE PAPER

All sorts of papers can be used in decoupage. You can buy paper specifically for this purpose in craft shops, but there are plenty of other options that will allow you to be far more creative and individual. Whatever you use, I suggest choosing papers of a similar thickness for each project as combining, say, thick photographs with thin napkins would lead to an uneven lumpy surface.

NAPKINS. Paper napkins are excellent for decoupage (see pages 47 and 49). Old-fashioned floral designs work brilliantly on furniture, especially when creating a distressed, faded look. I have found that napkins are the only paper to produce a good result for this look. Be sure to buy 2- or 3-ply napkins as it's only the top layer (the one with the image on) that you use.

COMICS AND MAGAZINES. Vintage magazines make great decoupage material. Magazines from the 1950s and retro advertisements all look fantastic when ripped up and used in this craft, while vintage pin-up images bring a glamorous iconic vibe to a dressing-table stool or drawer fronts. You can find all sorts of old comics and magazines at antiques markets and shops. Children's comics and illustrated books are ideal for covering children's furniture. As you'll see on page 251, I covered my little girl's bookcase in the pages from a secondhand Brambly Hedge book and it turned out beautifully.

BOOKS. Old text books with yellowed paper make a lovely backdrop for decoupage. I used my husband's old copy of J. D. Salinger's *The Catcher in the Rye* to cover my daughter's table and chair set (see pages 250–253). The book was missing pages so I didn't feel too bad about tearing it up, in fact it's a lovely way to preserve something that otherwise might be discarded as useless. Once the furniture was covered in text, I then embellished with little torn-up vintage flowers here and there.

CALENDARS. These are an excellent way of obtaining many images and prints for a small cost. You can find images of absolutely everything – famous artists' works, cars, cats, gardens, mystical images: whatever theme appeals to you. Calendars provided the images for our decoupaged bathroom wall (see page 103) – it's completely waterproof and makes for a really interesting and fun feature wall.

PHOTOGRAPHS. Decoupaging boxes with old photographs makes a perfect keepsake gift. I once made my mum a keepsake box for Mother's Day, covering it in old black-and-white photos of all the women, past and present, in her family on a backdrop of old letters, book text and faded flowers. Most of the people in the photos are no longer with us, so many happy tears were shed when she unwrapped the gift.

WHICH GLUE TO USE

PVA glue is ideal for the projects in this book as it's cheap and readily available in large quantities. You can also use Mod Podge glue to decoupage which is ideal because it contains a sealant whereas PVA does not. However, Mod Podge is more expensive, and as we'll be using varnish as a sealant, PVA is absolutely fine for our purposes. If you are decoupaging small items that don't warrant a coat of varnish, then Mod Podge is ideal.

You can use wallpaper paste if papering the inside of a cabinet; however, over time the paper will peel away from the surface. If you do want to use wallpaper paste, you'll need to prep the surface with a coat of diluted PVA glue first – use one part water to one part glue, and allow it to dry before applying the wallpaper paste (this gives the paste something to grip on to).

WHICH BRUSH TO USE

Paintbrushes do vary and the one you use can make all the difference. The really cheap ones with thick bristles can leave fine lines on your finish, which you can often see once dry. So if you want a really smooth finish, it's worth spending a bit of time (and sometimes a bit more money) looking for brushes specifically for varnishing that have soft, fine bristles. These are thinner too, so they don't load up with too much varnish. Also, buy two – a wider one for larger areas and a small one for the nooks and crannies. Make sure you wash them thoroughly in warm soapy water when finished.

WHICH VARNISH TO USE

POLYVINE LACQUER OR ACRYLIC DECORATOR'S VARNISH. These are both ideal for decoupaging and are available in gloss, satin and dead flat. Polyvine recommend using their lacquer for decoupage, particularly if you want a crystal-clear finish. If using acrylic varnish and you'd like a matt, hard-wearing finish, apply a coat of the satin finish first as it's thicker and stronger, and then finish with a couple of coats of the dead flat.

CLEAR, WATER-BASED POLYURETHANE VARNISH. This is also fine for most decoupage projects and does not yellow over time. I suggest using a clear gloss on your first coat because gloss dries completely clear and non-cloudy, then follow with a coat of clear matt varnish if you'd prefer a matt finish. If you only use several coats of matt, you may end up with a milky finish. Water-based polyurethane varnish is supposedly safe for food surfaces once cured but do check the label on your product, particularly if you are decoupaging furniture for a child.

BEST VARNISH FOR WALLPAPERED FURNITURE. After wallpapering furniture, rather than apply another layer of glue I recommend clear quick-drying Polyvine Acrylic Decorator's Varnish. If it needs to be hard-wearing, as on a coaster, table or wallpapered wall, apply their satin finish and then finish with another couple of coats of a dead flat if you prefer a matt finish. This is water resistant so ideal for bathroom walls, coasters and tables.

HOW TO DECOUPAGE

There are a few different approaches depending on what you want to achieve, so I'll take you through each one. Then when you decide on a project, you can refer back to this section for the appropriate instructions.

WRINKLING AND BUBBLING

Wrinkling and bubbling can occur during decoupage but there are ways to avoid this.

- Make sure the glue is not too thin or thick. You might need to add a little splash of water to your glue until it has a slightly thinner consistency and runs off your stirring stick.
- Don't stir your glue too briskly as this can create bubbles in the glue.
- If your papers will be overlapping (as in the tissue box project on the next page), using smaller pieces of paper will help avoid bubbling.
- When it comes to smoothing out air bubbles, a brayer is a very effective tool. Failing that, you can use a ruler or your finger.
- Whenever possible, allow a layer to dry before adding more layers of paper or glue on top. This is particularly important if your papers don't overlap or you're using larger pieces of paper.
- Don't be alarmed if your decoupaged piece does have air bubbles and wrinkles when it's wet. Most wrinkles and bubbles will disappear like magic once the paper dries and shrinks.

TECHNIQUE

STANDARD DECOUPAGE

If you use Mod Podge glue (see page 39) to decoupage a decorative item, like this tissue box, you won't need a varnish as it has a built-in sealant. But if you're decoupaging furniture or something that will get a lot of use, or if it needs to be waterproof, I'd highly recommend applying two or even three coats of varnish to make it really durable. For this project I used two different papers of similar thickness and some flower fairies cut from a secondhand book.

YOU WILL NEED

Object to be decoupaged
PVA or Mod Podge glue
Bowl
Stirring stick
Decorative papers of your choice
Scissors
Paintbrush
Brayer or ruler (optional)
Clear matt varnish (if needed)

STEPS 1, 2 & 3

Tip some glue into a bowl, then add a little splash of water until it has a slightly thinner consistency and runs off your stirring stick. Cut or tear the paper into pieces. I prefer torn pieces as these give a smoother finish with no hard, cut lines. Apply a thin to medium, even layer of glue to one area of the object then place a piece of paper on top and smooth it down from the centre outwards with the paintbrush, pushing any air bubbles out to the sides as you do. Repeat and continue until the item is covered.

STEP 4

When decoupaging onto a curved edge (like the tissue box opening), snip a few cuts into the paper to make it easier to wrap around the edge. Once the box is covered in the brown paper, allow to dry.

STEP 5

Apply the cutout fairies on top in the same manner and leave to dry before finishing the whole box with a final top coat of clear varnish, if needed.

TECHNIQUE

WALLPAPER DECOUPAGE

You will find examples of decoupaging with wallpaper in the wallpapered corner cabinet (see page 205), the old writing desk makeover (see page 201) and doll's house makeover (see page 261).

YOU WILL NEED

Object to be decoupaged
Wallpaper offcuts or remnants
Scissors
PVA glue
Paintbrush
Clean dry cloth
Brayer or plastic ruler
Clear varnish, such as clear quick-drying Polyvine Acrylic Varnish or clear water-based varnish

STEPS 1 & 2

Measure item and cut your paper to size (if you wish to make a template first, see step 7 on page 203).

STEP 3

Apply a thin layer of watered-down PVA glue (use one part water to one part glue) directly onto the furniture.

STEP 4

Line up the edge of the wallpaper with the edge of the object, then gradually lay it down. Smooth the paper out with a clean dry cloth from the centre outwards, removing any bubbles as you go by pushing them towards the edge. You could use a brayer if you have one, but a plastic ruler does the job just as well. Start at one end and run the brayer or ruler all the way down to the other end to remove bubbles. Even if some do remain, don't worry too much, as they will probably disappear once dry and even if they don't you won't even notice them. Leave for 24 hours until completely dry.

Apply two coats of clear matt varnish, letting the first coat dry thoroughly before applying the second.

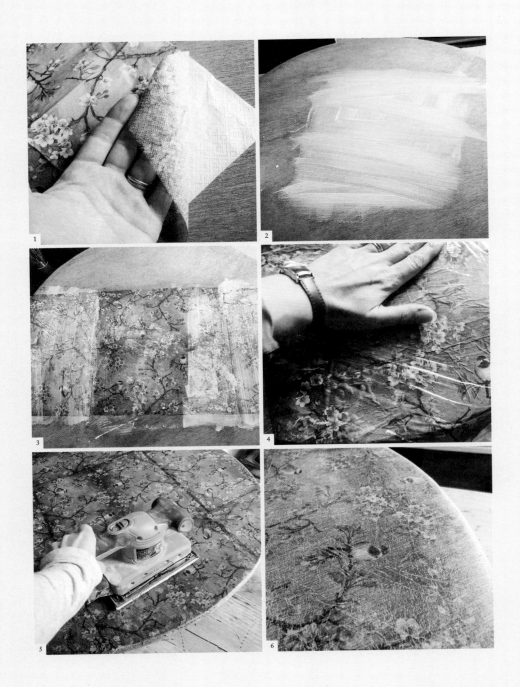

TECHNIQUE

FADED DISTRESSED DECOUPAGE

This is an easy but effective technique for transferring an image or pattern from a napkin onto wood. You can achieve this lovely faded worn look on any wooden surface provided it's porous and clear of paint and varnish, so give it a sand down beforehand if needed (see page 51). Napkins with brighter and bolder colours will imprint into the wood more visibly. Pale colours won't show up as much, which is fine should you want a more subtle effect, as in the Welsh dresser (see page 209).

YOU WILL NEED

Object to be decoupaged
3-ply paper napkins
Mod Podge glue (watered down to
  a runny consistency)
Paintbrush
Clingfilm (plastic wrap)
Handheld sander
Clear varnish, such as Polyvine Acrylic
  Varnish or clear water-based varnish

STEP 1

There are three layers to napkins but you need only the top one, otherwise this method won't work. They are tricky to peel so take your time.

STEPS 2 & 3

Apply a thin layer of watered-down glue directly onto the wood, lay your first layer of napkin on top, then gently apply another layer of glue.

STEP 4

Lay a piece of clingfilm (plastic wrap) over the top of the napkin. Then smooth it all down with your hand. This way you won't tear the napkin. Repeat this step all over the surface. Do not worry if it is covered with wrinkles and lines, this is all part of the effect. Carefully remove the clingfilm and allow to dry.

STEP 5

Once fully dry, use a handheld sander to gently sand and remove the surface layer of napkins which should reveal the faded image on the wood underneath.

STEP 6

Finish with two coats of varnish, allowing the first coat to dry thoroughly before applying the second.

TECHNIQUE

DETAILED DECOUPAGE

This is a lovely and effective technique for embellishing furniture, although it can be used to decorate almost anything. I recently cut out some adorable little flower fairies which I decoupaged onto a plain clock, and one of my favourite projects was cutting out these dainty flowers from napkins and decoupaging them on plain white eggs for Easter.

YOU WILL NEED

Object to be decoupaged
Paper or 3-ply napkins
Scissors
Mod Podge or PVA glue (watered
    down to a runny consistency)
Paintbrush
Clear varnish (optional), such as
    clear quick-drying Polyvine Acrylic
    Decorator's Varnish

Note: For these eggs I used Mod Podge glue because it contains a sealant and I didn't need to use a hard-wearing varnish. However, for a hard-wearing finish (for furniture or for a tray, for example), use either PVA or Mod Podge to glue on your paper, then finish with two coats of varnish.

STEPS 1 & 2

Cut out your design. If using napkins, separate the layers of tissue and just use the top layer.

STEP 3

Glue your design onto your item and apply a thin layer of glue over the top. When thoroughly dry, apply a final coat of Mod Podge.

SANDING

If you are interested in upcycling furniture, you will end up sanding at some point, by hand and by machine. Investing in a handheld electric sander is an absolute must, as it allows you to strip a piece of furniture down to its bare wood in no time at all. Some things you can sand by hand but stripping furniture by hand is not something I would recommend. I have used my electric sander countless times to strip coffee tables, kitchen tables, chairs, cabinets, bedside tables, cabinets... The list is endless and you can always guarantee a smooth finish.

THE ESSENTIALS
- Handheld electric corded sander
- Selection of high-grade sandpaper
- Protective goggles
- Protective gloves

WHAT TO LOOK FOR IN A SANDER

I have three electric sanders – two are heavy duty but the one I use the most for upcycling furniture is an electric corded compact mouse sander. These are extremely affordable and the triangular shape is designed to get into the nooks and crannies of furniture, making them ideal for this use. They often have extra little accessories for working on tiny areas.

Do make sure your sander has a removable dust collector attached, as sanders generate a lot of sawdust. Sanding is extremely messy work and even with a dust collector you are still likely to end up covered in sawdust from head to toe. This is why protective goggles and gloves are an absolute must, but emptying the collector regularly will help to keep the dust levels down. That said, do not let the thought of mess put you off. It's highly satisfying and absolutely worth it, as being able to sand furniture means you will be able to revamp and transform pieces, saving yourself an absolute fortune.

WHICH SANDPAPER TO USE

You'll need sandpaper for wood in various grits (or roughness). It's important to use good-quality sandpaper, as low-quality paper can affect your finish. There are sandpapers for wood and metal so make sure you buy the right one. Regarding the grit, the higher the number, the smoother the finish. If you're just starting out, and you want to remove a layer of old varnish you could use a low 40 or 60 grit, which is quite coarse and rough, then move on to 80 grit which is medium. The lower the grit, the quicker it should remove the layer. Then when you're down to bare wood and you want a smooth finish, move on to a finer grit such as 120 or 220.

- 40 grit: coarse
- 80 grit: medium
- 100 grit: medium

- 120 grit: fine
- 220 grit: fine
- 440 grit: extra fine

USING A HANDHELD SANDER

Using a handheld sander is pretty straightforward – put it on the surface to be sanded, turn it on and off you go. But there are a few things to consider if you want to get a smooth, even finish. I would often end up with annoying swirls etched onto my wood, but there are a few simple things you can do to avoid this happening. When you're ready to start it may be worth practising on a spare piece of wood so you can get a feel for the machine before starting on your final piece.

PREPARATION. Move your item into an open, well-ventilated area and put on your protective goggles, clothing and gloves.

HOLDING THE SANDER. You want an even pressure when sanding, so keep it straight and steady so it doesn't run away from you. Avoid tilting it or pushing it into the wood as this can leave marks.

SANDING. Place the sander on the wood and turn it on – this way you'll be less likely to mark the wood if it's already resting flat on the surface. Then move the sander along the surface in long, even strokes in the direction of the wood grain. Avoid going in a circular motion as this can result in those annoying swirls, and do work slowly. Going too fast will also result in marks and swirls. When finished, give the piece a good brush down.

SANDING BY HAND

Sanding by hand is easy to do, and it's vital to getting a smooth finish on painted furniture. The same rules as above apply in terms of different grits. When painting furniture, it will often need a light sanding before you start, and again in between coats of paint (once dry, of course). I like to wrap a piece of fine sandpaper of 120 or 220 grit around a small block of wood, as this makes it easier to hold when sanding by hand. Simply pop on some protective gloves and give the piece a light rub down in the direction of the wood grain (if preparing the piece for painting). If sanding in between coats of paint, sand in the direction of the paint strokes until the lines and ridges are smoothed out, then give it a good brush and begin the next coat of paint.

PAINTING FURNITURE

Painting furniture is an absolute game-changer and is by far the quickest and cheapest way to transform and furnish your home. Shop-bought painted furniture in the rustic style is incredibly popular but can also be very expensive. So upcycling an old, unloved piece of furniture will not only give you tremendous satisfaction, but you'll be saving yourself a lot of money in the process. On more than one occasion I've bought an old dresser in need of refurbishment for £20, only to see something similar already painted in the distressed style for £350! So if you enjoy painting and distressing and would like to make some extra money, painting to sell on is worth considering.

You may already know how to paint and upcycle but if not, it really is very easy. The next few pages may look like a lot of information to take in, but it's just a simple guide to each stage of the process. So dip in where and when you like, and we'll soon have you painting like a pro.

THE ESSENTIALS
- Undercoat or primer, if needed as a base layer
- Water-based furniture paint, to use as the main colour
- Varnish, lacquer or clear soft wax, for sealing and protecting the colour
- A selection of sandpaper (see page 52), for smoothing ridges or distressing
- Masking tape, for protection
- Paintbrushes, for painting and varnishing
- Lint-free cloth, for applying and removing wax

UNDERCOAT OR PRIMER?

I used to be quite lazy when it came to painting and I would often skip the priming/undercoating stage. I'd then wonder why my paint wasn't adhering to the furniture as it should. Some furniture paints don't require priming or an undercoat, but if they do, there's a very good reason for it.

You'd be forgiven for thinking a primer and undercoat were the same things but they do very different jobs. Primer is used on bare wood – it is the foundation that your paint will stick to (without it, the paint scratches off and marks very easily). The undercoat provides a neutral base and texture for the top coat of paint. If you have a dark wall and you're repainting it pale pink, you need a couple of coats of undercoat to transform the wall into a flat neutral colour, ready for a top coat of paint. If you're ever unsure which is which, just remember – if your surface is already painted, use an undercoat; if it is sanded and stripped back, use a primer first.

PAINT FINISHES

There are a variety of furniture paints on the market and it can be very confusing as to which one you should use. The best paint for you depends on the finish you like, so below is a simple guide. These paint finishes are now all available as water-based paints. Gloss used to be oil-based but now many brands sell water-based gloss, so do make sure you check before buying. Water-based is always preferable, as it has a much lower VOC content, it's quicker drying and doesn't yellow over time.

CHALK PAINT. Chalk paint looks matt and 'chalky' with a lovely finish, and it's very quick and easy to use as there's no need for sanding and priming beforehand. You can skip the undercoat and apply it straight to the furniture, so this is often a favourite product when upcycling furniture. Unlike some other finishes, chalk paint isn't washable and can mark easily, so using a furniture wax or lacquer to seal it is vital. These finishes are the most suitable for using with chalk paint.

EGGSHELL. Eggshell has a smooth texture with a subtle sheen. It is highly durable and hard-wearing, so ideal for furniture that is going to be well used. You can use eggshell on wood, metal and concrete, so it's great for furniture, floors, window frames and radiators. It does sometimes require an undercoat, especially if going from dark to light, but you don't always need a top coat of varnish.

SATIN AND GLOSS. Satin gives a mid-sheen finish to furniture, while gloss has a very high-sheen, almost reflective finish. Always check the can but most brands state a primer or undercoat is not necessary with either of these. You also don't need to apply a top coat of varnish, especially if using gloss, as it's highly durable.

THE IMPORTANCE OF PATCH TESTING. While there's no need to use a primer with chalk paint, it's always advisable to do patch test first. Whether you're using chalk paint or eggshell, the tannins of the wood can sometimes seep through the paint and cause yellowing, particularly when using lighter colours. Sometimes the yellow of the tannins doesn't show through until the top coat is applied so you'd need to do a patch test of both the paint and top coat to be sure, then leave it for a week or two as it can take a while for the tannins to show through. If you find the paint does yellow after doing a patch test you can apply a stain blocker such as Zinsser Bin to the item first, then paint and seal as normal. If you'd rather get stuck straight in, but you don't want to risk it yellowing, apply a stain blocker first to avoid any disappointment later. If you've already painted something and it has yellowed, simply apply the stain blocker on top, repaint with chalk paint and finish with a wax or lacquer.

WAX, VARNISH OR FURNITURE LACQUER?

When you have finished painting your furniture, it may require a top coat to protect it from knocks, spills and greasy fingers. There is nothing more soul-destroying than seeing a coffee-cup ring permanently fused into your newly painted side table. So don't skip the top coat. I always prefer a really natural, matt finish but there are a few options, so here we go...

FURNITURE WAX. Wax gives furniture a lovely natural finish and it is ideal for using on chalk paint. Coloured wax is my favourite thing to use on stripped bare wood (if I don't already like its natural colour) as it penetrates into the wood rather than adding a protective film on the top, and gives the most natural finish as it can be buffed up into a sheen or left as a matt finish. While the packaging usually states that wax does make the surface waterproof and stain resistant, I would only recommend waxing furniture that doesn't have too much contact with hands, pens and drinks. Wooden fireplaces, display cabinets, display shelves and chairs are all ideal for waxing. However, I wouldn't wax high-traffic items like coffee tables and sideboards unless you're an avid user of coasters and you're content to hover over your guests, playing coaster-police for the foreseeable future. Its protective qualities can be minimal and wear off over time, so it may need regular maintenance, but it's worth it in my opinion.

CLOTHS FOR WAX. You need a really soft, lint-free cloth for waxing. I've never bought cloths for waxing – I just use my husband's old T-shirts or my old leggings. As long as it's soft and lint free, it will do the job.

FURNITURE LACQUER. This provides a hard-wearing layer that seals and protects, and it's an ideal alternative to wax if you want a protective, water-resistant finish when using chalk paint. It used to be oil-based and come with a high sheen, but you can now buy water-based products with a matt finish. Like wax, lacquer penetrates the wood to form a seal and it has a very clear finish. But as mentioned earlier, be aware that when using chalk paint and lacquer, the tannins of the wood can seep through into the paintwork so a patch test is always a good idea, followed by a stain blocker if needed (see page 57). However, for items that require an extremely durable finish, such as children's desks or coffee tables, I'd opt for varnish.

POLYURETHANE VARNISH. This is a clear, water-based varnish. It comes in matt, satin or gloss and you can also buy a 'diamond-hard' finish for extremely hard-wearing surfaces. I use clear polyurethane matt varnish whenever I want a highly durable waterproof finish on decoupage projects. It does not yellow or lose its durability over time. Water-based polyurethane varnish is usually safe for food surfaces once cured but always check, particularly if painting children's toys or furniture.

POLYVINE PRODUCTS. Polyvine make brilliant products for numerous craft projects. Polyvine wax-finish varnish is one of my favourite products as it has the protective qualities of varnish but in a natural wax-like finish. I once used it to seal some painted peg dolls I made for my daughter Frankie – they have been well used and three years later there's not a single scratch on them, so I know it's durable. It's ideal for using on wood and painted furniture. I haven't used it on chalk paint but I know many do. Polyvine also recommend their lacquer for decoupage, particularly if you want a crystal-clear finish. Polyvine Acrylic Decorator's Varnish is a clear varnish that has UV protection and can be used to protect paintwork, emulsion and wallpaper from marks, fingerprints and scuffing. Most of their products are available in gloss, satin and dead flat.

WHICH PAINTBRUSH TO USE

Paintbrushes will make all the difference to your finish. Avoid very cheap brushes with thick bristles as they will leave fine lines on your finish, which you will see once dry. I'd also recommend having separate brushes that you use for painting, varnishing and waxing, rather than using the same brush for all jobs.

ROUND BRUSHES. When it comes to painting furniture with chalk paint, my absolute favourite brush is Annie Sloan's round brush (I have one for painting and another for waxing). They may seem expensive compared to others in the DIY shops but they are absolutely worth every penny (I put them on my Christmas and birthday list!). They really go the distance and give an excellent finish. Round brushes are popular for using with chalk paint because they are so versatile. There are a variety of techniques you can do with them to create different textures, including cross-hatching, feathering, stippling, dry brushing, frottage, wash and ragging. I want to keep this guide fairly simple so I won't go into how you achieve each one, but it's definitely worth trying a few of these techniques as you grow in confidence.

BRUSHES FOR VARNISH, WAX AND A SMOOTH FINISH. If you're looking to get a smooth finish when painting, use a medium brush that has soft, fine, tapered bristles. Get a selection of different sizes too, as it'll take all day if you try to paint a large table with a tiny brush, and you'll need a small brush for the nooks and crannies. Always use separate brushes for varnishing and waxing too. Varnishing brushes are often wide but thinner so they don't load up with too much varnish. Previously I used a lint-free cloth for waxing, and I sometimes still do for applying wax to shelves, but when it comes to waxing furniture I always use a round brush. It's so much easier to use and I prefer the finish.

CLEANING BRUSHES. Whatever brushes you are using make sure you clean them thoroughly. If your products are water-based then cleaning brushes with warm soapy water is ideal, just keep washing them until there is no residue left. Otherwise they'll dry hard and end up too stiff to be used. I don't use any oil-based products in these projects but if that is what you are using, you'll need to clean your brushes with white spirit.

PAINT ROLLERS. If you have quite a big piece of furniture, or perhaps you're painting drawers or a cabinet, using a roller is an option. It is quick to apply paint with a roller and you can get a really smooth finish using a small, high-density foam roller. Foam rollers are preferable to flocked rollers as flocked have tiny hairs that can leave a textured finish on your surface, as well as the occasional hair.

MASKING TAPE

Get a good-quality easy-peel masking tape especially for decorating. Preparing before painting is the best thing you can do for yourself, but it's the step people often skip. Putting masking tape on windows, skirting boards (baseboards) and furniture is the most boring of tasks, I know. But if you skip this step you will be cursing yourself later as you spend hours painstakingly scraping the excess paint from your window with a butter knife. Peel off the masking tape when you have finished painting but before the paint has dried (if you pull it off afterwards, this may result in the paint coming off with it).

HOW TO PAINT FURNITURE

Here is a straightforward guide to painting furniture from start to finish. I prefer to use chalk paint for painting furniture as I love the finish and it's so quick and simple to use. However, I have also used other paint finishes in this book so you'll be able to see the different approaches. In this guide I'll include all the various steps and you can find more information on each product used earlier in this chapter too. You can also learn how to use two or more colours, to create depth in the frottage chairs on page 193, which is a lot of fun to do. Once painted, it is incredibly quick and easy to make newly painted furniture look old and shabby using distressing techniques (see pages 65–67).

PREPARE PAINT. Give your paint a good slow stir to dispel air bubbles (if instructed to on the can). Paint straight from the can or pour into a small container. I like to tip my paint into a small plastic container as it's easier to hold and if I stop for a cuppa I can put the lid on more easily. If your paint is very thick you can add a little water to thin it out slightly, although I'd suggest trying it first as it may be fine as it is.

PREPARE FURNITURE. Move your furniture into a well-ventilated area. Remove any hinges, door knobs and accessories unless you plan to paint them. I keep mine separated in little cups to make them easier to put back.

SAND. If your paint surface is uneven, give it light sanding to smooth out any bumps or ridges – this also helps the paint stick, although do note that sanding isn't necessary when using chalk paint. When finished, give it a wipe down to ensure it's completely clear of dust.

PRIME. If your paint doesn't require a primer or undercoat, hop straight to the next step. If transforming something light you may only need one coat of primer. If it's dark you may need two or three. Work the primer into the wood with a brush or roller, then leave to dry. Apply in the same manner that you plan to paint, for example if you're going to paint using long, smooth even strokes, apply the primer in the same fashion. Once the first coat is dry, give it a very light sanding with a fine sandpaper such as

220 grit, dust and then apply the next coat of primer. If you're painting the hinges, don't forget to give them a coat of primer too.

PAINT. Dip your brush into the paint so a third of the brush is covered, then wipe the excess off on the side of the can. You don't want to overload your brush, as too much paint will lead to an uneven texture. Whatever brushing technique you use, avoid pressing too hard as that will add brush lines. Also, don't overwork an area too much, so keep moving. If the paint starts to feel tacky don't go over it, as this will cause drag marks.

PAINTING FOR A SMOOTH FINISH. If you'd like a smooth, sleek finish, apply the paint to the surface using a flat brush. Hold the brush at a 90-degree angle, and move it back and forth in long, even strokes, in the direction of the wood grain. Allow it to dry and give it another coat. If using chalk paint, you can also water down your paint a little to make it go on smoother.

PAINTING FOR A RUSTIC FINISH. If you'd like a more natural, rustic finish that perhaps you plan to distress, apply the paint using quick strokes, back and forth, moving the brush in all different directions as you paint. I find a round brush works much better for this technique.

FEATHERING. Once you've got an area covered, do some light feathering over it. This is when you sweep the paint lightly with only the tip of the brush. This reduces brush marks and can be done in one direction or every which way.

SECOND COAT. Allow your first top coat to dry. If you're happy, move on to the second coat; if there are any lines you'd like to smooth out, give it a very light sanding and apply the second coat. If you want to distress your furniture once dry, carry on reading.

DISTRESSING FURNITURE

Starting with the main edges of the furniture, begin running your sandpaper along the edges, back and forth until you begin to wear the paint away and you have the desired effect. I usually use a higher grit such as 220 for a softer, distressed affect and a lower, coarser paper if I want to take quite a bit off. Depending on the thickness of the paint, you may need to rub a little harder in some places. Gradually work your way around the piece.

If you have long edges you can run a putty knife along the edge, or hold a butter knife at either end and scrape it along the edge, then give that edge a light sand as you don't want splinters. You want this effect to look natural, so wear out the areas that might wear naturally – edges and corners – making some bits more distressed than others to avoid a uniform look. Pick out any interesting or ornate details too, on the furniture and on the hinges and door knobs. This can really bring it to life.

You can use a handheld electric sander for distressing. Take the same approach as above and run it along the edges lightly, then use fine or medium grit sandpaper on the corners and detailing, as a sander can be a bit heavy-handed for those areas. If you haven't had much experience with a sander, I'd suggest using sandpaper for distressing until you're confident. They do the same thing in the end.

FINISHING OFF

FINISHING OFF WITH VARNISH OR LACQUER. All products vary so read the tin for advice on application. You want smooth, even coverage with minimal lines, so take the same approach that you did for painting, in other words light feathery strokes. If an item needs a lot of protection, allow it to dry and give it a second coat.

FINISHING OFF WITH WAX. Waxing can be done before or after distressing. Give the item a good dust, then apply the wax with a brush, or a soft lint-free cloth (an old T-shirt is fine). I prefer waxing with a round brush that I keep solely for this purpose. Cover the brush head in wax and sweep it over the paint, until the whole piece is covered. Think of it like applying moisturiser after a shower! If there's any excess wax left behind, give it a very light wipe with a lint-free cloth. Either leave to dry as it is if you'd like a matt finish, or, if you'd prefer a light sheen, buff the wax with a clean cloth 24 hours later. Just buff the wax away (as if you are removing it) and you'll start to see and feel it become velvety smooth and shiny.

AGEING FURNITURE WITH WAX

While browsing furniture shops, have you ever wondered how they make pieces of furniture look so old, faded and shabby? And how you can sometimes see more than one colour peeking through too? This is very easy to achieve using a two-tone colour technique which can really give furniture some added depth, as well as allowing us to play with colour. I use this technique on the frottage painted chairs on page 193. Once the paint is dry, to make it look old and antiqued, use a clear wax followed by a dark wax. It might look dirty when it first goes on but once buffed off, it ages furniture perfectly.

APPLY CLEAR WAX. Apply a layer of clear wax to the whole piece. It's important to give it an even coat of clear wax before you go near it with the dark wax.

APPLY DARK WAX. While the clear wax is still wet, apply the dark wax a little at a time. Don't worry if it looks quite dark, just get it on there using a brush or a lint-free cloth. Really work it into the detail of the wood, going against the grain, getting it into all the nooks and crannies.

CLEAN OFF WAX. Once the dark wax is applied, begin cleaning it off with your cloth. You'll see it will have ingrained itself nicely. Take off as much as you like, and if you'd like to remove more you can use some clear wax which acts as an eraser. Take it back a little at a time until you are happy with the finish. Leave it to dry overnight, then give it one more final coat of clear wax to seal it.

ORGANISING YOUR SPACE

A BEAUTIFUL HOME IS AS MUCH
ABOUT FUNCTIONALITY AS IT
IS ABOUT AESTHETICS

This chapter looks at how we can make the bones of our homes work more efficiently for us, by clearing space, making space and also using space more creatively.

We'll begin with clearing space through decluttering. You might be wondering what decluttering has to do with crafting a beautiful home, but I'd say everything. A beautiful home is as much about functionality as it is about aesthetics. There are people who aren't bothered at all by mess and clutter – they can live happily among it and just go about their day. Some people even thrive when surrounded by sky-high piles of organised chaos. I'm envious of them if truth be told as it must be liberating not to be ruled by your inner Monica, instinctively tidying as you go.

My mum is an organiser (apple and tree, I know). She would always make the house look immaculate when guests came to visit, but I started to notice that even once they had arrived, my mum would still continue to work hard, waiting on them, tidying away as she went, and when they left she was exhausted. We'd all tell her to sit down and relax, but she just couldn't help herself, which made me realise there is definitely a balance to be struck. We want a lovely, organised home so that we can then be free to live the life that we want to live, rather than live-to-tidy. As a result I now have the house prepped and ready to go for my guests, but once they arrive I hang up my gloves and relax. It's not easy for me, I have to consciously check myself as my instinct is to constantly 'clear', but as well as considering my own well-being, I'm also thinking of my daughter Frankie. She'll be watching me just as I watched my mum, and while it's pleasing to have a tidy room, it's also important to be in the moment and enjoy life as it is happening.

DECLUTTERING

Decluttering involves getting rid of anything you don't really want or need. Easier said than done though, isn't it? Many of us find it hard to part with things because 'I might use that one day', 'I looked great in that dress in 1998', 'I can't face sorting it'… So instead we tidy up and stash what we don't want to see out of sight – under the bed, at the back of the closet and in the loft it goes. Our living space might look clear and tidy for a short while, but it is a temporary fix, especially when it turns out that a lot of the things we have stashed are things we do use and need on a regular basis. So then we can't find them and buy them again. If you are in this rut, it's probably time to tackle it head on.

If you have no clutter whatsoever, and you have ample storage for all of your things, then I am high-fiving you right now. You can give yourself a pat on the back and move on from this chapter as you are likely to be the minority here, since most of us mere mortals carry some kind of baggage, myself included.

LETTING GO

You may have attempted to declutter before, and perhaps it hasn't worked because you are too attached to certain items on an emotional level. I think a lot of us can relate to that. I'm incredibly sentimental, and I'd often struggle to get rid of things. So I had to alter my perspective and a friend recommended reading Marie Kondo's book *The Life-changing Magic of Tidying*, which I found very useful. I didn't take on all of Marie's advice (I did attempt to fold and store my underwear vertically for a while, but it didn't last), but a lot of Marie's teachings did help to change my outlook for the better, and I was able to let go of things more easily. If you struggle with letting go on an emotional level, or you just want more help tackling clutter, I highly recommend it. I can only scratch the surface with a few paragraphs here. Such things do warrant some expertise and a whole book.

TIPS FOR DECLUTTERING

BE IN THE RIGHT MOOD. This is probably the most crucial thing, isn't it? Feeling ready and willing to purge. If you're tired or feel upset it's probably not the day for a clear out. I often have a day within my cycle when I just want to clean, so when I wake up in that place I'll capitalise on it and use it as a window of opportunity.

GET HELP IF NEEDED. If it's a struggle for you physically or emotionally, bring in reinforcements. Do make sure they're the right person for the job. My mum is my ideal clear-out partner – she's patient, we like similar things and she understands the process. If I did it with my husband he'd probably get bored quite quickly and just tell me to chuck everything. Your partner and/or kids may want to declutter with you, because it is likely to be their stuff you're throwing out too. If you think it will work well, by all means go for it. If you think it's likely to end in a battle of wills, it might be sensible to go through the process alone. Then when you have made the piles listed below, you can discuss and go through each one. If they don't agree at any point, items can always go in the 'second chance' pile.

PACE YOURSELF. Give yourself time to declutter your home, when you don't have any distractions. If you try to do everything in one afternoon, you'll end up getting overwhelmed as it can be a messy, chaotic business. Depending on how much stuff you have it may be something you work through a chunk at a time. One category over a weekend perhaps? It's better to do one category thoroughly, than merely skim through the lot.

THE APPROACH. You might prefer to do one room at a time, or like Marie Kondo recommends, one category at a time, for example starting with clothes, books, papers, miscellaneous items and finally, sentimental items. Marie starts with clothes because they're the least sentimental. You take every single item of clothing you own and put it in one huge pile. This way you're able to see accurately just how much you own, and you'll probably be more inclined to let some of it go. The approach in a nutshell is this: you take an item in your hands, and ask yourself 'does it spark joy?'. If it doesn't make you feel any kind of happiness or joy, let it go. (I'm not sure my glue gun sparks joy, but I know I still want it, so this question might not always apply!) Also, once you've cleared out your wardrobe and are left with just the things you love, you'll see proof of your efforts every time you open the door and it will encourage you to move on to the next stage.

CATEGORIES OF CLUTTER

When it comes to having a clearout there is quite a lot you can do with your unwanted goods. So think about what your categories could be. Here are some examples; you could pick just three or use all of them.

KEEP. These are things you absolutely love, want, use and need. The things that make you happy, and that make your life easier. Does it spark joy? If the item doesn't do any of the above, it goes.

SECOND CHANCE. I don't use this category but you might need it. This is for 'I don't want to give it away so I'll keep it for six months and if I haven't used/worn it by then, it goes' items. Set an alert on your calendar for six months. Do not be tempted to put all your things in this category – it is to be used in an emergency when no decision can be reached.

SELL. Anything that's worth selling at an auction, car boot, garage sale or online goes in this pile. If you're going to sell it online you could take a photo of it there and then, and if it's clothes also take a picture of any measurements or details, such as the brand. It will save you doing it again at a later date.

REHOME. This is my favourite thing to do. If you're struggling to part with something, perhaps a gift from a loved one but you just don't use it, ask yourself if you know someone who might like it? Knowing it is going to a good home to be loved makes all the difference. I recently had a sort out of Frankie's baby things. Oh my goodness, I sobbed! There was so much of it but I felt a surge of relief when I thought of giving it to a good friend who was just weeks away from having her baby.

CHARITY. Another favourite. Giving to a charity or clothes bank is always a win-win. You get rid of things that someone else really needs and will appreciate. If your clothes are in great condition they can go to charity shops/thrift stores and clothes banks. If the clothes are damaged, stained or have holes, you can put them in the textile and fabric recycling bin. But be aware that on more than one occasion I have picked up a dress in a charity shop, declaring 'Oh that's just lovely!', only to realise I was the one who dropped it off there a week before.

RECYCLING BIN. Finally, for the broken objects that are at the end of their life, put these in the pile for the rubbish or recycling centre. These places are incredible, and often have an area for selling things too, so you may grab a bargain while you're there.

ORGANISING

So now we've decluttered we can get stuck into organising. If you are an avid organiser like me, you probably get just as excited over a good bit of storage as you do about a weekend away. Well, maybe not that excited but it's close, right? It is a good feeling when everything finally has a place, and finds its way back to that place regularly. When our homes are a well-oiled machine, we tidy less, we are less stressed and we are free to do more enjoyable things.

So first let's assess what storage you do have, then if it's not enough, we can consider ways of creating more. Most of us are in need of more space and storage, so decluttering first is always ideal. Then we can really see what we're dealing with, and create permanent homes for things as opposed to quick fixes.

EVERYTHING IN ITS RIGHT PLACE

Before creating more storage, let's look at what you already have. Pick a room that has already been decluttered and try the following. Open all the cupboards and drawers and just take it all in. The first task is to find permanent homes for the fundamentals. So look at all the fundamental things in the kitchen. Are they in the ideal spot? You want to be able to move swiftly and easily around your kitchen, and where things are kept can really affect that. For example, is the kettle near to the kitchen sink and are the mugs close to the kettle? Are the butter knives near the toaster? Are the dinner plates and cups you use all the time in an easy-to-reach cupboard? Look at those fundamentals and if it's not ideal, have a change around.

DECLUTTER. If you haven't already decluttered your kitchen, do that first. It will make organising a lot easier. Read tips for decluttering on page 73, get some boxes labelled for the things going to recycling and so on, and empty one cupboard at a time until every cabinet and drawer contains only things you want to keep.

READY TO ORGANISE. If everything feels like it's already in a good spot with just a few things needing to be swapped around, then by all means just move those items. But if you feel that actually quite a lot of it could probably be in a better place, try this approach. We'll start with cupboards, then move on to drawers.

EMPTY YOUR CUPBOARDS. Empty your cupboards into a space in the middle of the room – whether it's onto the kitchen table or floor doesn't matter, just don't empty onto the worktops, as we'll be using those in a minute. Keep food items grouped if they were already together, and make sure you leave enough room around it all to access all cupboards. (Yes, it's going to look like a bomb has gone off, but take a deep breath, it will be worth it!)

CLEAN THE CUPBOARDS. When everything is out of the cupboards, give them a good clean.

REORGANISING. Now slowly start to find new homes for everything, starting with the fundamentals. Get the cooking oils, herbs and sauces near to the cooker, place the knives near the chopping boards and veg basket, house the packets of teas near the mugs and kettle and slowly work your way around, giving everything a permanent home. If space is limited, and there are things that you use only seasonally (a slow cooker in winter or an icecream maker in summer), rather than take up valuable space, pop them in a box and stash them when you pack away your summer/winter clothes. That may sound odd but when it's time to get out your chunky knits in autumn you'll also be ready to make some warming stews, so it makes perfect sense! When all the fundamentals are in the right space, start finding homes for everything else. If you become get stuck and you find there is just not enough cupboard or drawer space, put what is left to one side for now. Make a cup of tea, take a breather and read the ideas over the page for creating storage and making space.

SHELVING

Creating shelving is an excellent way of making more storage space. I've made shelves for most of the rooms in our house and it is incredibly easy to do. It is also much cheaper than buying 'off the shelf' (excuse the pun). In the kitchen we have handmade chunky scaffold shelves, while in the bedrooms there are small vintage shelves with little ornate brackets. Our next project is to put up a live-edge shelf in our living room (a live-edge shelf has a raw uncut edge on one side, which can be a lovely feature and a great way of bringing nature into the room too).

DISPLAYING THINGS ON OPEN SHELVES

We put up several shelves in our kitchen and use them to house the things that are attractive and in daily use, such as crockery, potted herbs, pestle and mortar, and so on (while the less attractive but essential items such as plastic food containers, condiments and cans of food stay out of sight in the cupboards).

If you've run out of cupboard space but have plenty of blank walls, you could create a gorgeous wall pantry. Decant rice, pasta, flour and cereals into glass storage canisters and you'll free up a world of room for other things in your cupboards. You can buy clear printed labels for such food items now too. If I had more wall space, I would absolutely fill it with such things. Even very small shelves are useful for housing and organising items such as dried herbs, egg cups and kitchen knick-knacks.

You'll find step-by-step instructions for making shelves on page 85.

HOOKS

Oh, the humble hook – how underrated it is! Such a small thing, but what a difference hooks can make to a home. They can be used everywhere, for so many things. Where there is no room for a shelf, you can guarantee you will find places for hooks. And the more we can hang, the less we have on the floor, stacked in piles or stuffed in drawers.

You can find a variety of hooks for different jobs; the pretty ornate cast-iron ones for when on show, the cheap but sturdy screw-in hooks for when they're not, and the clear plastic ones that can be stuck on if making a hole isn't an option. Some of these suggestions might sound obvious initially but you'd be surprised, because it's not always about where you hang a hook but what you put on it that can make the difference between chaos and order! Hopefully these ideas will enable you to create more homes for things, making your daily life easier and your home a lot more organised.

HOOKS ON DOORS

BEDROOM DOOR. Ideally we want the bedroom to be a calm and uncluttered environment. So while we don't want to treat our door like a clotheshorse, more than one hook might actually lessen the appearance of clutter. We used to have a single hook on our bedroom door and every morning I had to wrestle with it, bleary eyed, in a bid to untangle my dressing gown from everything else! When we put up two pretty cast-iron hooks side by side, it was such a small change that made a big difference.

CHILD'S BEDROOM DOOR. A great place for multiple hooks! My little girl only had one hook at the top of her door, which was useless to her considering she's just 60 cm (2 feet) tall. So I installed a row of pretty hooks across the middle of her door that she could reach. Ideal for her dressing gown, fairy wings, swords and the huge array of handbags she is currently collecting. If space is limited in a child's room, this is also a great place to hang an organiser with compartments for all their little bits and bobs.

HOOKS ON WARDROBES. If there is enough depth in your wardrobe or closet, the inside of the door could be an ideal spot for a row of hooks to hang handbags, scarves and hats. You could even have two or three rows of hooks with hats at the top, then scarves, and handbags on the bottom. If it's a squash though, don't do it. The last thing you want is a cluttered wardrobe with a door that won't close. Instead, could the same arrangement work down the side of the wardrobe? Another simple but pretty way of displaying costume jewellery and delicate scarves is to hang an ornate hook and pop a pretty triangular coat hanger on it (I like using antique wooden ones for this purpose). Then you tie or drape your scarves over the bar, or attach your jewellery.

INSIDE CUPBOARD DOORS. Airing cupboards, kitchen cabinets and utility-room doors could all be working harder than they are. You can buy heavy hooks which you can fix to the door on which to hang your ironing board, which is a great way of getting it tidied away. Hooks on the inside of utility cupboards are useful for hanging all sorts – think bags for pegs/clothes pins, rattan baskets, wall organisers and first-aid kits.

BACK OF THE KITCHEN DOOR. Again, a great place for a few well-placed hooks and ideal for things you want access to every day – mine houses my large straw shopping bag and my wooden broom (which keeps it close to hand and out of a cupboard). It's little touches like this that can also make the kitchen feel homely.

HOOKS ON FURNITURE

HIDDEN HOOKS ON FURNITURE. If you have a dressing table or an area where you dry and style your hair, screw a hook on the side of the dressing table, hidden from view. Most hairdryers have a hanging hoop so it's an ideal way of keeping your bedroom things organised and off the floor. I also have hidden hooks (self-adhesive plastic ones) under my bathroom sinks on which I hang a cleaning cloth for giving the sink a quick wipe down.

UNDER UNITS. A great one for the kitchen and bathroom. If you have kitchen wall units or shelves, make use of the space underneath. Even if the cabinets are laminate or MDF, you can still screw a row of hooks to hang your mugs. My hooks hold eight mugs, which frees up quite a bit of cupboard space. Of course, I use them to hold my favourite mugs so they look pretty too! If the hooks are hidden under the unit, cheap metal screws will work, just make sure they're big enough to hold your mug handle.

UNDER SHELVES. Hooks under shelves are incredibly useful, especially in the kitchen. Plus, if you're going for that rustic, cottage-kitchen vibe, this will help you achieve it. If the hooks will be visible it's worth getting some lovely wrought-iron ones.

HOOKS ON WALLS AND CEILINGS

HOOKS ON KITCHEN WALLS. Hanging a rail with a row of hooks on can be a great place to hang utensils. In my kitchen I have a wrought-iron pole with hooks on which I hang crockery, utensils, little copper pans, measuring spoons – all useful things we use every day. It looks great, and also saves us searching in drawers.

HOOKS ON BATHROOM WALLS. Hooks in a bathroom are very handy and can prevent the room becoming a jumbled mess. Hanging wall hooks within easy reach of the bath can be a lovely feature, ideal for hanging sponges and brushes, making bathtime a little easier and more luxurious.

HOOKS ON THE CEILING. If you love the country-cottage style and you have wooden beams or slats on your kitchen ceiling, you can easily hang quite a bit up there. I have copper pans hanging from our ceiling (the more mundane non-stick ones are in the cupboard), but I hang baskets and dried herbs from the ceiling too. If you create ceiling hooks, make sure they're secure and screwed into solid wood with no chance of falling. If you're worried about weight, lighter baskets and herbs are a great alternative.

MORE ORGANISING TIPS

USING DRAWER SUB-DIVIDERS. This is an excellent way of avoiding the doom of the jam-packed drawer. Decide which drawers are for what, then work through each one, giving everything its own permanent home. It may be a time-consuming job, but it's so worthwhile. Small plastic food containers are ideal for separating household items such as batteries, elastic bands and glue.

TIERS IN CUPBOARDS. Creating a tiered step system in a cupboard is brilliant because it allows you to see and reach items easily. I've used this method in my food cabinets for a while now. You can buy tiered shelf organisers, or simply get a few lengths of wood, cut them to the cupboard size and stack them to create steps (three at the back, then two, then one).

STORAGE TROLLEY. If you have an awkward narrow space between two units that's not big enough for a cupboard, park a storage trolley in it. I've done this with a three-tiered trolley that's currently filled with bulky dried goods such as bags of pasta and rice, and the rice cooker. I made a simple curtain (see page 141) that covers both the trolley and the dishwasher, and you'd never know they were there.

THE LAZY SUSAN. A lazy Susan is so useful. I use one on the top shelf of the fridge for condiments (be careful of things getting cluttered around it), but they're also ideal in cupboards for small items such as jars of herbs.

BAKING TRAY ORGANISERS. Baking trays are another awkward thing to house. The clatter alone is frustrating when you're wrestling a baking tray out of the cupboard and the rest of the cupboard contents fall out with it. Head online and search for a baking tray 'file' that allows you to slide out the one you want. You can find similar organisers for pans, too.

CLEANING CADDY. A two-tiered under-the-sink organiser for cleaning products is a great way of using up dead space. Couple that with a little caddy that attaches to the inside of the cupboard door for things you use daily and clearing up will be a doddle.

SPICE RACKS. Rack holders are brilliant for fixing to the inside of a cupboard door if you're short of space. If you can't screw holes, you'll easily find strong self-adhesive ones available.

PAN LID RACKS. Pan lids can be a pain as they're awkward to stack and can take up a lot of room. So fixing a pan lid rack to the inside of a cupboard door is a great solution. Just make sure it's big enough for the majority of your lids.

PROJECT

HOW TO MAKE A SHELF

Making your own shelf couldn't be easier. You can pick up scaffold boards secondhand if you want a chunky shelf, or buy a smooth piece of wood from your local DIY shop, then you simply choose brackets to fit the depth of the shelf. When it comes to wax or varnish, research the various shades of colour before choosing, as there are many. Before deciding on your style of shelf, do make sure it's suitable for the wall you're hanging it on as not all walls can take the weight of a heavy, chunky shelf.

YOU WILL NEED

A piece of wood
Paint scraper and wire brush
   (optional)
Handheld sander
Wax or varnish
Paintbrush or lint-free cloth for waxing/
   varnishing
Shelf brackets

STEP 1 - CUT SHELF TO SIZE

You can do this yourself if you have
a good saw. If not, either ask someone
to do it for you or enquire at your local
hardware shop.

STEP 2 - SAND THE WOOD

Remove any dirt or lumps with a paint
scraper and wire brush, then sand all
the edges and both sides of the shelf
using a handheld sander, especially if
it's a chunky scaffold board. You want
an even pressure when sanding, so

keep it straight and steady. For detailed
instructions on using a handheld
sander, turn to page 52.

STEP 3 - WAX OR VARNISH

If the shelf is for a bedroom or living
room, furniture wax is fine. If it's going
in a kitchen or bathroom where it's
likely to come into contact with water,
think about using a matt varnish or
lacquer instead.
- For wax, give it a coat of furniture
wax using a wax brush or a soft lint-
free cloth (an old T-shirt is fine). If you
prefer a matt finish, leave it to dry as
it is, or for a light sheen, buff the wax
away with a clean cloth 24 hours later
and it will become velvety smooth.
- For varnish or lacquer, give it a coat
of varnish/lacquer in the colour of your
choice (or clear), and opt for matt if
you'd like a more natural wood look.
Allow it to dry, then repeat.

LUGGAGE AS STORAGE

Wicker picnic baskets, old trunks and vintage suitcases make excellent storage because they can hold quite a lot and they make a great feature when stacked, whether your vibe is cosy-cottage, retro-vintage or modern. Keep an eye open for them at car boot sales or garage sales, and in charity shops and antique shops. Here are a few ideas for using them.

- A trio of wicker picnic baskets stacked up works brilliantly in any room of the house. I have some in my craft room containing all sorts of craft paraphernalia, and a further three stacked in the living room to hold a variety of Frankie's toys. I put pretty luggage labels on each one so we know what is inside, and as the baskets are lightweight they're easy to manoeuvre and their handles mean they can be transported easily.

- A stack of vintage suitcases or wicker picnic baskets makes a quirky little side table when placed next to a sofa, with a lamp popped on top. These are ideal for storing long-term items you don't need regular access to.

- Large trunks make very characterful coffee tables, while also providing a great storage spot for board games, photo albums or winter throws when not in use.

- If you have the room, a large trunk at the foot of the bed makes a great alternative to an expensive ottoman, for housing blankets, duvets and spare pillows.

- Large wicker trunks make ideal toy boxes for children, as the lids are lightweight and easy for them to open, and they won't break little fingers if slammed shut.

- A couple of vintage suitcases on top of a wardrobe make a great style feature while also using empty space. I have photographs and summer/winter hats in ours, and again, they'll work with a rustic or modern style of room.

CREATING SPACES

You'll be surprised by what you can create in the smallest of spaces with just a little thought. Repurposing areas for yourself or your family members can be especially useful if you live in a smaller home, or perhaps you have a growing family with ever-changing needs. So giving a space a dual purpose can really maximise what you already have. Once you've had a good clear out and found homes for the rest of your belongings (see pages 72 and 76–83), you may find it frees up room you didn't even know you had. An old airing cupboard, an unused shed or the area under the stairs are all ideal candidates for a multi-use transformation.

This is the story of how we transformed our dumping ground under the stairs into a library and secret hideout!

BRAINSTORMING THE SPACE

The space under our stairs was slowly becoming a dumping ground. It had some shelves which housed books, but other than that the space was filled with stuff: the vacuum cleaner, account folders and some leftover cans of paint. It was an area that I would clear regularly, but because it was an empty space, things just accumulated there again and again, and I loathed it. Most of us have that one cupboard or that one drawer that we despise opening, and this was it for me. Initially I thought of making a curtain to cover it all up, but the space had potential. So I found new homes for everything, gave it a thorough clean, and then I sat it in and had a good think about how we could best use the space.

The shelves meant a mini library was a must. I then toyed with building a storage cupboard for the vacuum cleaner and shoes, but then I thought of Frankie. She is still little, and there is something about nooks and crannies that young kids just love. They could have a beautiful big playroom but show them a slither of space behind the sofa, and that's where you'll find them. So why not make it a little secret den for her and her friends to play in? I can use it for shoe storage when she's a teenager, plus it would be an opportunity to house some of the toys that were gradually taking over the living room.

PAINTING THE SPACE. The stairs are in a corner of the snug, which is currently a light grey-beige (Farrow & Ball Shaded White), so I opted for a deep burgundy (Farrow & Ball Brinjal) for under the stairs. If you want to make a space feel bigger, lighter shades are ideal, but I wanted to keep this a cosy, cave-like space and the burgundy contrasted beautifully with the grey. I gave the sloped ceiling a coat of blackboard paint, so Frankie and her little friends could enjoy drawing on the ceiling.

LIGHTING THE SPACE. The main ceiling light doesn't illuminate the area under the stairs very well, so I bought a string of plug-in copper fairy lights (battery-operated would also work well) and wound them round a length of faux ivy and nailed it all to the edge of the wall using cable pins, following the edge of the ceiling and winding them around the post to finish. I didn't want Frankie and her friends to trip over the wire so I taped it to the floor with a wood-effect floor tape.

FLOORING. I wanted some cosy cushions for the kids to sit on, but just chucking a pile of cushions on the floor would have made it quite cluttered. A long oblong floor cushion was ideal, but this would have been expensive to buy. I then remembered I had six square seat pads that I wasn't using. I had bought them for my kitchen chairs but they were the wrong shape – it turns out that a square cushion on a round chair seat can be incredibly frustrating to sit on, so it was time for an upcycle treatment!

HOW TO MAKE A FLOOR CUSHION. I arranged the seat pads on the floor in three sets of two. Then I sewed extra cushion ties on any sides where they were needed, using the whip stitch (see page 32). This meant I could tie them all together, but take them apart easily when they needed a wash. A long cushion like this fitted my space perfectly but soft fluffy rugs are also ideal for hangout spaces. Just make sure they're washable, especially if children or pets will be using the space.

ACCESSORISING. The fun bit! Frankie chose a flower fairy picture to hang on the wall and we added some bunting under the fairy lights. Frankie decided it would make a great cafe, so in went her kitchen (a great move as it was getting a bit cluttered up in her room). We added her picnic basket of play food, her menu, books and teddies, and 'Frankie's Cafe' was open for business.

Frankie and her friends absolutely love playing in her den, and drawing on the ceiling is a big plus point. But aside from it being a fun place, it's also the first place she runs to when she's cross or upset, providing a safe space for her just to be in.

When we're invited to the cafe we often sit in there and have a read of our books or look through our photo albums while waiting for our 'food' to be served. It's wonderful having a place dedicated to our books, and as there are quite a lot I have organised them by subject. I have even bought little brass label holders to write the categories on, so when family and friends visit they can enjoy a browse in the 'library' too, while enjoying a cup of tea in 'Frankie's Cafe' of course.

WALLS AND WHAT TO DO
WITH THEM

WHEN IT COMES TO SOURCING THINGS
FOR YOUR WALLS, THE ONLY OPINION THAT
REALLY MATTERS IS YOURS

What we put on the walls and how we decorate our homes can have a profound effect on our well being and our daily life. Our homes should ideally be a place of warmth, a sanctuary from the outside world that we can't wait to return to. But inevitably life, work and commitments get in the way, and the sanctuary we longed to create gets put on the back burner. In no time at all you might find you are struggling with clutter – not necessarily unwanted clutter, just things you haven't yet found a home for. Perhaps there is a colour on the walls that you don't particularly like, but you're living with it for the time being. Maybe the photos or artwork on display don't spark any joy in you, or perhaps you simply haven't got around to hanging any pictures.

When you realise that this is the case, it pays to take a step back, pick one room and, as always, take it one step at a time. Making a home, or a room, really work for you doesn't always need to be a huge undertaking, it just takes a bit of time and, more importantly, some thought.

GETTING STARTED

The first thing to tackle is your belongings, by getting rid of anything you no longer want or need, then finding or making permanent homes for the items you want to keep. Tackle this most crucial stage by using the information in the Organising Your Space chapter on page 69. But for now, let's fast forward to decor.

If you are decorating a room and are trying to decide on colours/style/design, the question to ask yourself should never be 'Is this on trend?' or 'Would my followers like this on social media?', because if you base your decorating decisions on the answers to those questions, the results will not be a true reflection of you, and you will not benefit from your living space. Instead, ask the simple question 'How do I want to feel in this room?'. In a bedroom you might want to feel peaceful and serene, or perhaps you want it to be a sensual and sumptuous space. In a kitchen you might want an open, warm and friendly feeling, or you might want it to be chic, industrial and stylish. Each of these directions will inspire different decor choices, and aside from creating the perfect space for yourself, by using your aspirations as your guide (rather than those of online trendsetters), you will open your mind to options you may not have considered before.

A ROOM FOR EVERYONE

If you have a family and everyone will be using the room, be mindful of what kind of space would be beneficial to them as well. If you let this be your guide, you will ultimately end up with a room that will make you all feel good.

Our surroundings need to support and enhance our daily life so be realistic when planning ahead. Striving for a chic, white, minimalist design with two toddlers and three dogs running around is going to be an uphill struggle for you. You want your home to improve, not hinder, your day-to-day life, but that's not to say you can't use that minimalist blueprint somewhere else in the house, a bedroom or a bathroom perhaps?

WALLS AND COLOUR

It is truly incredible how a lick of paint can completely transform the look and feel of a room. Sometimes it's glaringly obvious which colours will work in a room, but at other times it can be frustratingly difficult. I've learned a lot about colour, albeit mostly through making mistakes, and it has opened my eyes to possibilities I wouldn't have entertained before. Here is an example of just that, along with the valuable advice I was given along the way.

Our living room had one sage green wall (a shade I usually love) and oatmeal cream on the others. Although I liked the colours, I kept hanging pictures, shelves and photos on the walls but nothing ever seemed to look or feel good to me. Regardless of how I lit the room, even in ambient lamplight everything just felt a little lacklustre and bland. So I decided on a change of colour. I bought some sample pots of colours I thought I liked and slapped them on the wall. It turns out this was my first mistake, and here's why.

DO NOT PAINT SAMPLES STRAIGHT ONTO THE WALL. This is not a good move for many reasons. Firstly, the Pigeon Grey you paint on one wall can, and usually will, look completely different on all the other walls in the room. It's remarkable what light and shade do to colour. So to get an accurate idea you would have to paint your sample on every wall you plan to paint. Then if you want to try five other samples you are going to end up with a patchwork of swatches on all your walls. It will become very confusing, not to mention making your wall patchy prior to painting. Instead, paint your sample onto a large piece of white paper or card, then pin it to various walls, behind sofas and under pictures, because it really helps to truly see a colour when it is against or behind something else. Spend time with each colour, looking at it at various points in the day, as it will change constantly.

USE A COLOUR WHEEL. Many paint companies provide colour wheels of their shades which are incredibly useful, and can cut out the stage of painting samples on paper, as above. Although you usually have to pay for these, they are much bigger samples than the little colour cards you can pick up free of charge. It may seem like an unnecessary expense but trust me, it will save you a fortune on sample pots and you will use the colour wheel time and time again. If you're unsure of colours, I recommend you get one.

SEEK ADVICE. Despite picking samples of all the colours I really liked, none of them seemed to work for my living room. It is quite a big, light space, and the subtle muted colours I was choosing seemed to look very washed out on the walls. So, I called in the cavalry. Many paint companies offer an hour-long colour consultation service, either virtually or in person, and a lovely person from Farrow & Ball came to my aid. The consultant takes on board your likes and dislikes, and makes suggestions, drawing on their expertise in colour and light. This can be an expensive, albeit worthwhile, service so it may not be an option if you are on a budget but what it taught me more than anything else was to expand my palette of colours.

OPEN YOUR MIND TO ALL COLOURS. For our living room the Farrow & Ball consultant suggested Inchyra Blue, which is deep and dark and more teal green than blue – a colour I initially wouldn't have considered. I was originally looking at a plaster pink paint shade, but after seeing the sample held against my furniture and artwork, I absolutely fell in love with it. It made everything in the room pop, from the artwork on the walls and the shelves to the furniture.

GO WITH YOUR INSTINCT. While it's useful to get the opinion of a colour consultant/your friends/your mother-in-law/the milkman, none of them has to live with the colour on a daily basis. It's very easy to be influenced by someone else's vision and we can end up committing to something we're not entirely convinced by. A consultant is incredibly helpful if you're undecided, but for one of my other rooms my consultant recommended a lovely muted colour. I already had a colour and vision in mind for that room, but I chose to go with her suggestion instead. Once painted, I knew straight away I should have stuck to my initial instinct. Because while it looked perfectly fine, it wasn't what I envisioned and it didn't make me feel anything. When it comes to your home and how it makes you feel, there is no opinion more important than your own.

PAINT TO YOUR BUDGET. There are some beautiful, quality paints available nowadays, and some companies charge a pretty penny for that can of paint. If your budget won't stretch to the high-end brands, then you can try to colour match. Find the expensive colour you like and get it colour matched at your local paint store. However, bear in mind that when it comes to colour you do sometimes get what you pay for, as the top-quality companies use technology that gives their paint real depth. If unsure, get samples of both. You can always mix and match – use the posh paint in the rooms that you use the most, and colour match elsewhere.

FEATURE WALLS AND FIREPLACES

In many rooms, there is often one area or a single wall that lends itself to being the focal point, or feature wall. Having that focus in a room really helps to create balance as it becomes the central point and you can work everything else around it. A fireplace in the living room is always a great focal point, but all too often it's the television that takes centre stage, with furniture angled towards it. You'll have a much nicer space if the television doesn't dominate the room so try an alternative focus – a mural or a beautiful wallpapered wall can draw the eye, as can a decorative mirror or artwork. Couple that with a wooden shelf or beam across the middle of the wall, and you have a focal point that you can dress for every occasion with seasonal flowers and decorative objects.

FIREPLACES

If you're lucky enough to have a working chimney, then a fireplace makes the most wonderful focal point. If the chimney has been sealed up, bringing it back to its former glory is often easier than you may think. In our previous home the fireplace had been blocked up and plastered over. It was a rented property but our landlords were happy for us to work on the house, providing we were making improvements. We created a fire surround with two upright wooden beams on the sides and a third beam laid across the top, and we knocked through the plaster to reveal an existing fireplace. The job was done in one day with the help of my dad (who knew what he was doing – always seek the help of someone who is skilled in these structural matters). I then used a rustic plaster to finish the front, bought a fire grate, had the chimney swept and we were warming our toes just a few days later.

The cottage we live in now has two fireplaces so I consider myself very fortunate. Both are very different. The snug fireplace looks no different to how it would have done in 'the olden days', as my little girl would say.

The living-room fireplace has a log burner, set in a square alcove. While it looked perfectly fine sitting within its plain plastered wall, I wanted to frame it, and make it even more of a feature. So we painted the room a beautiful deep teal (Farrow & Ball Inchyra Blue) and sourced a fire surround from the local reclamation yard. I loved its shape but it was grubby and needed work. I sawed a section from each leg so it framed the fireplace equally on all sides, then sanded it and finished it with a coat of wax. It really gives the room a wonderful focal point and added balance to the wall as well.

FRAMING WITH HOPS. Hanging a garland of hops is a wonderful way to frame a window or fireplace. There is something so wonderfully sweet and homely about them with their frothy green flowers and heady scent. The garland never fails to transport me to Ma Larkin's bustling kitchen in *The Darling Buds of May*, the first in a series of books about a family living in rural England in the 1950s, written by H. E. Bates.

You can buy beautiful, thick hop garlands from garden centres or from hop specialists. The bonus of buying one ready-made is it will arrive boxed, with ties on the back, ready to hang. I bought the one that hangs above our fireplace, but then I started to notice hop vines on our daily dog walks, growing thick and fast in the surrounding hedgerows. I have since cut lengths from the hedgerows, and I even discovered some growing on the front of my house! Once you become familiar with hops you will always spot the vines when in bloom.

The vines are much easier to handle when fresh (albeit a little sticky), but you can gather a few strands together to make a garland and then fix it in place so the garland can then dry where it hangs. If you buy a ready-dried garland, do have the vacuum cleaner handy when you are ready to hang it because it will make quite a mess! If hanging above a fireplace, do make sure it's hung securely and is a safe distance from the fire.

PROJECT

DECOUPAGE BATHROOM WALL

If you fancy creating a feature wall without the expense of wallpaper, a decoupage wall is a brilliant solution. It costs very little money to do and is easily achievable. I created this wall in our cottage bathroom – a small room with a pretty little window overlooking the garden.

Initially, I went onto autopilot and set about creating a tranquil, spa-like room with white walls, pale muted colours and white fluffy towels, but then it occurred to me that this room could provide a good opportunity to inject a little fun and colour into the house. I looked around at the existing decor of rich dark blue tiles around the bath and a vibrant sunshine yellow on the outside of the bathroom door and immediately thought of the Norfolk coast. The beautiful beaches and quaint little seaside towns have retained that old-fashioned nostalgic atmosphere depicted in vintage postcards and it was that feeling I wanted to capture in this room.

I began by painting the walls white and the side of the bath a warm shade of yellow reminiscent of sand (I used Hay by Farrow & Ball). I sanded the windowsill and the wooden floor back to their natural shade and gave them a coat of suitable varnish. To add the wow factor, I decoupaged an entire wall in colourful vintage travel posters, featuring places from all over the United Kingdom. To order individual prints would have cost a small fortune, so I had the idea of buying vintage calendars! I ordered three different calendars so I had more than enough images to cover the wall. The whole family loves it. It is colourful without being overwhelming and there is always something interesting to rest your eyes on. The wall makes me think of sunny days and the seaside adventures that lie ahead.

Calendars are an excellent source for this project because you can find images of your favourite artworks, travel destinations, animals, flowers and botanics. Just let your imagination run with it and see where it leads you.

YOU WILL NEED

Filler (optional)
Fine to medium grade sandpaper
Several calendars of your choice
Scissors
Blu-tack
PVA glue
Bowl
Water
Stirring stick
Paintbrush
Plastic mat or wallpaper pasting table
Cotton cloth
Clear matt waterproof varnish

STEP 1 - PREPARE WALL

Give the wall a good clean. Fill in any holes
with filler and smooth out any bumps using
fine to medium sandpaper. *See picture: top.*

STEP 2 - POSITION IMAGES

Cut out all your images and pop a tiny
blob of Blu-tack on the back of each. You
could skip this step and start gluing the
images straight to the wall, but I recommend
having a play around with them before you
commit them to their final position. If the
images are varied, arrange them so they
work well together – for me that meant
making sure there weren't too many of the
same colours grouped together and aiming
for an even balance of colour throughout,
with busy images interspersed with the
simpler ones. I also experimented with their
alignment, choosing whether to align them
vertically or have them staggered. I started
by tacking them to the wall and standing
back to review, then moving and swapping

WALLS AND WHAT TO DO WITH THEM

images one by one until they flowed well. I positioned them from left to right on one row, then right to left on the next so the edges were always varied. You may need to cut some images along the edges to fit. *See picture opposite: bottom.*

STEP 3 - FINAL ARRANGEMENT

When you're happy with your positioning, take them down again in the correct order, starting from the end and working backwards – this will allow you to put them up one at a time in the right order.

STEP 4 - PREPARE GLUE

Mix up a large bowl of PVA glue and water it down until it is a runny consistency and it runs off your stirring stick easily. If it's not runny enough, it will be prone to bubbling. You could use wallpaper paste, but I want the decoupaged wall to last and wallpaper paste is more prone to peeling.

STEP 5 - GLUE IMAGES IN PLACE

Lay your first image face down on a mat and cover the back with a thin, even layer of glue using a paintbrush. Pick up the pasted image and lightly position on the wall. Smooth it down with the cloth working from the centre outwards in every direction, pushing any bubbles to the edges. Don't worry too much if any bubbles do show up, as they should disappear once the glue has dried.

STEP 6 - COMPLETE WALL

Continue the step above until every image is on the wall and allow it to dry for 24 hours.

STEP 7 - VARNISH

When dry, give the entire wall three coats of waterproof varnish, allowing each coat to dry thoroughly before applying the next.

MIRRORS

Mirrors can be an incredibly useful and powerful tool when used in the right way. They can really open up a space, but they can also magnify an ugly one if we're not careful.

SOURCING AND UPCYCLING MIRRORS

You can buy mirrors from most homeware shops, but I've sourced my favourite mirrors in secondhand shops. You can find really unusual and original mirrors in antique shops (in fact, I recently bought a lovely hammered copper mirror in my local antique shop), although you may have to pay a higher price.

However, you can often find gorgeous antique mirrors in car boot sales, garage sales and charity shops for far less. I've bought many inexpensive mirrors simply because I liked their ornate shape, even though the gold or brassy colour of the frame did not appeal to me. These mirrors make excellent upcycling projects. Making over a mirror is very simple – just pick any one of the sample paint pot projects in the Furniture Makeover chapter on pages 186–213 and apply the same instructions to your mirror frame. Using two colours can really give the mirror some depth and interest too, and if there's intricate detail you can highlight this when distressing.

WHERE TO PLACE MIRRORS

There might be obvious places to hang mirrors in your home, but before you jump in, it is worth taking a moment to give it a little more thought.

While it may seem a world away from my style of cottagey decoration, I've been intrigued by the ancient Chinese practice of feng shui, which focuses on the placement of objects and how they affect the energy (or chi) in the space around us. The aim is to harmonise individuals with their surrounding environment. A lot of it is based on common sense, and I've always found its pointers on mirrors to be particularly useful (see below). By all means, take on as little or as much of this as you like. If you're in doubt, have someone hold the mirrors for you and try them in a variety of positions.

AVOID HANGING MIRRORS ABOVE THE BED OR SOFA. Feng shui experts warn against heavy objects hanging over or above you as it's important to feel fully relaxed and safe in your space. If there's a big, weighty mirror/artwork/shelf suspended over your head, chances are it's going to affect your ability to relax fully, even on an unconscious level.

PLACE MIRRORS OPPOSITE A BEAUTIFUL VIEW. The idea is to bring about positive energy so if possible, reflecting light and beauty back into the room is a win-win. Often we hang a mirror without really thinking about what it will be reflecting or magnifying. Placing a mirror opposite a shelf stacked with paperwork and clutter isn't going to add anything positive to the room, but reflect a pretty shelf, a lovely view, a selection of plants and you're enhancing the positive. Next time you pass a mirror, have a look to see what it is bringing back into the room, and if it's not a positive view, is there somewhere else you could try hanging it that would bring about a better aspect?

AVOID HANGING A MIRROR OPPOSITE A DOORWAY OR AT THE TOP OF A STAIRCASE. A mirror opposite a doorway is not ideal as it reflects the energy that is flowing into the room straight out again, rather than allowing it to flow in and around the room. The same applies to the staircase – if you have a mirror at the top of the stairs, any positive energy flows up the stairs and straight back down.

AVOID HANGING A MIRROR OPPOSITE YOUR BED. Most of us have mirrors in the bedroom and that's fine, but what can really disrupt sleep and the flow of good energy is if we hang them in the wrong spot. We need the bedroom to be a restful space, but if there is a mirror opposite your bed, you're likely to be startled by movements reflected in it, which can also make you alert, trigger adrenaline and disrupt your sleep. This makes sense to me as I know I'd be creeped out by a mirror hanging opposite my bed (I've seen too many spooky movies!). Instead the best place would be on a wall that is not facing the bed or doorway.

EXPANDING SPACES. Sometimes it's nice to celebrate small, cosy spaces, rather than feel the need to make everywhere appear bigger, but if you do have cramped areas such as the landing or a downstairs loo that you'd like to make feel spacious, mirrors certainly can help. Place one on the top half of the wall alongside a loo (rather than directly opposite it) and it could double the space. You can also be clever with mirrors in terms of directing energy around the house. It might help if you imagine energy to be a breeze that you're helping to flow around the house, so a mirror at the top of a staircase would boomerang it straight back down the stairs, whereas a mirror on the staircase wall halfway up would help send the energy into the landing in the upper part of the house.

BEING TOO SELF-AWARE. This is based on my own perception of how mirrors can affect us, mentally and physically. If you have a large mirror in your living space, you'll notice that the first thing you and your guests probably do upon entering is look at your reflection. Mirrors have a way of pulling us out of the moment so that we can check ourselves – our teeth, our hair, our wrinkles, our figures. It can become compulsive. For that reason I haven't hung a large mirror in our living room as I like the fact that when we're in there, we are not face or body aware at all. It makes for a more relaxing existence. We do have mirrors in other rooms but they don't greet you face-on. In fact, there is only one full-length mirror in our house, so if you want to see your whole self, you have to go looking for it.

It's worth noting the impact mirrors may have on children too, particularly if you have older children who may be struggling with their appearance for any reason. If you have a large mirror opposite your shower and it makes any of you feel negative in any way, get it out of there (and if you can't remove it, paint it). You'll notice the difference instantly.

FINDING THE RIGHT MIRROR

Finding the right mirror for a particular place can send you on a wild goose chase. I will admit that I have a stash of gorgeous mirrors. Some women collect shoes; I appear to be collecting mirrors. This wasn't intentional, I might add. I bought the majority of them to hang above one of our fireplaces but I just couldn't find the right one, so one mirror turned into, well, quite a few! This was a real learning curve for me, so I thought I'd share my accumulated knowledge.

PROPORTIONS. You need the right size of mirror for the space, but this isn't as obvious as you may think. Often people think bigger is better, perhaps because they're trying to open up the space, but if the mirror is disproportionately big, it will overwhelm the wall and dwarf everything around it, which might actually make the room look smaller. Like everything, balance is key. The first mirror I bought was too big, and it made my wall look cluttered.

SHAPE. This is an important one to get right. Remember the lovely hammered copper mirror I mentioned on page 107? I thought that was going to be a winner. It was the right size, it was an octagonal mirror and it just looked wrong. I realised that the wall was already full of hard angles with an oblong window, a square fireplace and a shelf. This wall didn't need more edges; it was crying out for curves. Here is a very simple and much cheaper solution to establishing the best size and shape of mirror for your space – simply cut various sizes and shapes from newspaper and pin them to the wall!

COLOUR AND STYLE. The next contender was a pretty, curvy, oval antique mirror with a cream frame. But despite the curves being an improvement, the colour was not working, nor was the oval shape nor the style. It was too 'shabby chic' and that was not what the room wanted at all. It was at this point I finally realised what was required: a simple, small round antique brass mirror. I searched online and in secondhand shops and I finally found it!

ARTWORK

Finding things to hang on the walls that work with the room, happily sit alongside all the other pieces in the space and make us feel good can be tricky. But the great thing about rustic cottage interiors is that they perfectly lend themselves to a slightly ramshackle quirkiness. Nothing needs to match, it's a jumble of this and that and anything goes. Well, that's what it looks like on the surface!

When it comes to choosing artwork, sometimes we end up with things on the wall that don't actually make us feel anything. Perhaps you've just stopped seeing it there, perhaps it was a gift or you chose it because the colours suited the room. If you're not feeling inspired by your wall art, it's time for a change. Sell the unloved pieces or send them to the charity shop and let's start over, because having photos or artwork on the walls that make your heart sing is going to make all the difference to your daily life.

The joy of art is that it can move us in some way when we look at it, but even as I'm writing this I realise I need to take my own advice. I'm looking at a print that I recently hung in our living room and I'm not moved by it at all. I liked how the colours worked against the wall colour, it is pretty, but that's it. It has been there a month and I don't think I've even looked at it twice, so I'm clearly not benefiting from it. In contrast, I look at the painting on the other wall almost daily, I want to dive right into that one. So the other picture will come down today.

CHOOSING ART FOR EVERYONE

When it comes to choosing things for your wall, the only people whose opinions really matter are those who will be looking at it. It's certainly not easy pleasing everyone, but it would be preferable if the people you live with also like the artwork you choose to display. If you have an image hanging in your dining room that your children or partner despise, they won't enjoy spending much time there, and it can negatively impact their daily life. So while you might be the person sourcing the artwork, try getting family members involved in it too.

If you love a piece which they don't, perhaps it could be hung in your bedroom or a place they don't wander into often. Likewise, if you're thinking of choosing something that's a bit risqué it's worth bearing your visitors in mind too, for both your sake and theirs. While you might love having a painting of a naked woman displayed above your fireplace, will you also feel at ease and comfortable when your father-in-law drops in for a cup of tea? If you feel uncomfortable at the thought of seeing him red-faced and choking on his biscuit, then perhaps save that painting for your bedroom too.

SOURCING ARTWORK

Finding artwork needn't be an expensive business. You probably already have some lovely pieces lying around your home without realising it. Here are some ideas and some crafty ways of making your own works of art.

ORIGINAL ARTWORK

We have original artwork by several artists hanging in our home. Some I found in antique shops, some were bought from art galleries and some were created by friends and family with artistic talent. My Uncle Titch (his actual name is Brian Seymour) is a very talented professional artist and he gave us a beautiful artwork. I was going to frame it but I just love the simplicity of it as it is. My friend Tina created the most incredible sketch of Ralphy, our dog and my friend Penny did some amazing paintings of Brambly Hedge imagery for Frankie's nursery. I am lucky to know such talented, generous artists. There are artists everywhere; you might even know some yourself.

Supporting and championing artists is such an important and worthwhile thing to do, and the bonus is we can enjoy their imagery on our walls every day. Even if you can't afford to buy original pieces, you can buy original prints of artwork which is much more affordable. Commissioning someone to do a sketch of your mother's dog or your sister's baby would make a very special gift indeed, while also keeping a small business, and its artist, afloat. If you're keen to buy original artwork, you could start by searching for local artists in your area, or take a wander to your nearest gallery. It won't be long before you stumble upon something you love.

VINYLS. My dad gave me his collection of classical vinyl many years ago, each record sleeve adorned with a different work of art. I fell in love with one of them, so I transferred the record to a plastic sleeve and sacrificed the cover. I cut out the artwork and put it in a rustic picture frame, and it's still hanging on my wall, all these years later.

Vinyl records also make great works of art themselves. If it has a cover you love and music you love, your appreciation for it is on an even deeper level. You can buy little wooden slats that you can pop on your wall to display the album. We have one above our record player, so the sleeve of whatever is being played on the stereo stands proud on the shelf. If choosing records to hang as a display, perhaps choose albums that promote feelings of positivity in you, rather than those that might leave you feeling wistful or melancholic.

BOOKS, MAGAZINES AND CALENDARS. Books are great places to source artwork. If you're looking for artwork for a child's room, you can find some incredible full-sized illustrations and imagery in children's books. Head down to your local library and browse, or simply search online for beautiful children's illustrations. Then you can either make a high-quality photocopy of them or buy an old, possibly damaged secondhand copy of the book. I find gorgeous illustrations all the time just through reading to Frankie but I've run out of space on her walls.

Keep your eyes peeled when flicking through magazines too, or if you are looking for something specific (such as nature prints or vintage posters), you might find just the perfect images in a calendar. I once found an incredibly majestic image of a pheasant in a nature magazine (he looked just like Hopson, the pheasant who visits our garden), so I cut it out, put it in an antique frame and gave it pride of place above the old fireplace.

PHOTO WALLS

Photo walls are a brilliant way of celebrating precious memories, and of making a house feel like your home. If you live in rented accommodation, try using the excellent sticker hooks you can now buy, as these won't damage the walls. I have photos in almost every room of our house as there are so many moments to remember and so many faces I want to see regularly. A photo wall is ideal as it allows you to hang a good number of photos while also creating something visually special on your wall.

CHOOSING PHOTOS FOR A PHOTO WALL. The key to creating a photo wall of absolute joy is not choosing photos based on how good you look. Instead, choose photos based on your emotional reaction to them. If a photo gives you a positive reaction – a genuine smile, a laugh, a warm glow – it's in. If not, move on. This is worth trying, because we might think that certain memories are happy ones but without realising it, sometimes photos actually evoke emotions such as nostalgia (photos of the good old days) or sadness (photos of loved ones no longer with us), and some can leave us feeling wistful or mournful (photos of ourselves in our youth perhaps, rocking a snakeskin boob tube and stilettos on top of a bar in 1996).

Personally, I love having photos of my departed loved ones nearby, but I don't always have them on a photo wall if I still feel a great sadness when I see their faces. Instead, I'll either have them in a photo album or on a different shelf that I can go to when I want to see them. Because while all these people and memories deserve to be celebrated, you don't want to be put through emotional turmoil every time you walk past your photo wall. You'll be missing out on feeling the positivity and love this wall could potentially bring you.

Whenever I'm having a particularly hard time, I'll go to my photo wall. I just spend a few minutes with the images, looking at those memories, at the faces of all my most favourite people, and I just feel their comfort. It soothes me, and I'm OK again. As always, make this for you and your family's benefit, no one else's.

CREATING A PHOTO WALL. There are endless options for photo walls. You can design it by colour, by buying or painting all the frames the same hue. You can opt for uniformity by using identical or similar frames. You can align the frames into a neat grid design, or have them placed randomly. Personally, I'm all about mismatching – my photos are different sizes and the frames are a variety of styles and colours.

Even if you're going for that mismatched vibe, there are still a few tricks to getting the photos to sit happily together. One of the keys to a good photo wall is having a standard amount of space between the frames, regardless of how they are arranged.

First, let's look at the layout. Once the photos are in the frames, lay them out on the floor, then play around with the arrangement until you find one that you think works. Perhaps start with your centre point, with the bigger, heavier frames towards the middle or bottom centre, and work your way up and out from there. You could try standing on a chair and looking down on the layout when doing this. This stage is crucial because if you just start nailing them to the wall, I guarantee you will end up with a wall full of holes. Bitter experience has taught me this!

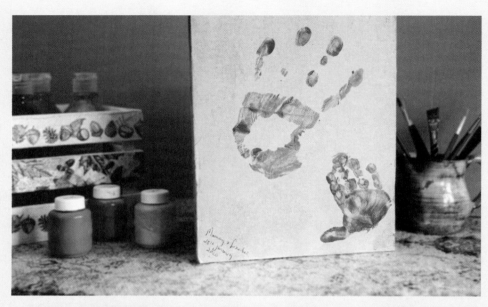

PROJECT

DIY ARTWORK

This is a great way of displaying and preserving something for your wall. You could use children's artwork as shown here, or it could be memorabilia from a special occasion such as your wedding invitation, or simply a picture that you love. This was the first handprint Frankie made with paints. She didn't like the feeling of cold paint on her hand. Her fingers were pressed tightly together, and I love that the moment is visible in her hand print! So rather than frame it, I decoupaged it onto a block of wood to hang on our photo wall.

YOU WILL NEED

A piece of wood, roughly the size
  of your artwork
Vice and saw (optional)
Sandpaper (optional)
Mod Podge or PVA glue
Paintbrush
Artwork of your choice
Lint-free cloth
Clear matt varnish (optional)
Two screws
Screwdriver
Picture wire

STEP 1 - CUT WOOD TO SIZE

If your sheet of wood is not cut to size, either ask the hardware store to do it for you, or if you have the tools and experience you could cut it yourself using a vice and a good saw. You'll then need to sand and smooth the edges.

STEP 2 - APPLY GLUE

Water down the glue just a little, then apply a thin, even layer to the wood. Lay the artwork on gently, then use the cloth to smooth it down from the centre outwards, removing any bubbles in the process. Brush another thin layer of glue on top. Allow to dry.

STEP 3 - VARNISH

If using Mod Podge there's no need to do an additional coat with varnish as Mod Podge contains a sealant. If using PVA, give the artwork a couple of coats of clear varnish to seal, allowing the first coat to dry thoroughly before applying the next.

STEP 4 - READY TO HANG

Once dry, screw the nails into the back on either side with the screwdriver and tie on some picture wire, ready to hang in your chosen spot.

A LOVE OF LINENS

ON A FUNCTIONAL LEVEL, SOFT FURNISHINGS
BRING WARMTH AND COMFORT TO A ROOM,
BUT ON A STYLISTIC LEVEL THEY CAN
REALLY TRANSFORM IT

There are certain things I always gravitate towards when shopping, with linens coming top of the list. Cushions, blankets, rugs, soft furnishings – we just love them, don't we? Many of us cover every possible surface with them – beds, sofas, chairs, floors – and while most of these things serve a useful purpose, it can be a little harder to justify the presence (or quantity) of others. My husband is not a big fan of cushions, for example; he complains regularly about the number we have adorning our sofa and feels the need to remove them before sitting. I have no idea why, as their primary function is to cushion! However, I do resist the urge to layer up the bed with lots of ornamental cushions (throw pillows), because even if they look wonderfully inviting, I don't need the extra task of removing and replacing them morning and night, and one or two on a bed can do the same job as eight.

On a practical level, soft furnishings such as blankets, bed linen and cushions bring warmth and comfort to a room, but on a stylistic level they can really transform it by softening edges and adding colour and pattern, as well as bringing balance to a room by using different textures such as velvet, faux fur, wood and hessian (burlap). If you are the kind of person who likes to change things up quite often, playing with soft furnishings is key. You might find it useful to keep your walls fairly neutral or muted so you can bring solid colour into your surroundings through furniture (such as a sofa) which will allow you to play with colours, patterns and textures through your cushions and other soft furnishings. This allows you to change your colour palettes and style as often as you like.

I love to adapt with the seasons, in both colour and texture. In autumn our living-room cushions are swapped for warmer hues and the thin cotton summer crochet blankets are changed for soft sumptuous chunky knits, while in the bedrooms warm, richly coloured bedspreads replace the fresh, pale green summer ones.

FABRIC DYEING

When it comes to buying fabric for cushions and curtains, whether new or secondhand, do remember you can dye fabric. So if you find some long white curtains that are just the right size and price, but aren't quite the right shade of duck egg blue for your home, dyeing may be the answer. Always dye a little swatch first so you know you'll be happy with the result.

DYEING WITH NATURE

I seldom dye with shop-bought colour. I prefer to dye with natural ingredients if possible as the colours you can achieve can be really beautiful, ranging from subtle, barely-there tones to bolder hues – it's an art in itself. You can create vibrant yellows, dusky pinks, rich terracottas and azure blues simply using flowers, vegetables, plants and bark. If you're interested in dyeing in this way I recommend getting a book on the subject as there's so much that can be achieved – it makes me feel like a nature witch, stirring ingredients into my cauldron (well, bucket)!

DYEING WITH CHALK PAINT

Some branded chalk paint (such as Annie Sloan) can be used to dye fabric too, although I've not yet tried this myself. I'm told it works particularly well on antique cotton and linens, less so on polyester. Bear in mind the colour results will vary depending on how much water you add – less water means a stronger colour, while diluting the paint more results in a lighter, more washed-out effect. A patch test is definitely worth doing.

DYEING WITH COFFEE

One surprising product I have achieved excellent results with is instant coffee. It's a very quick process and always works perfectly. It can transform a white lace panel into a gorgeous shade of antique gold and I've used this technique a lot. I learned this trick from the dressmaker who made my wedding dress, as she dyed the underskirt with coffee to match the antique lace of the dress.

- Wash the garment so it is clean and oil free. There's no need to dry it after washing as you can pop it straight in your coffee bath.

- Fill a bathtub, large sink or bowl (whatever size you need for the quantity of fabric) with very hot or boiling water.

- Tip in a whole jar of instant coffee (or two if it's a big bath) and stir until fully dissolved. Drop in your fabric and let it steep. If you want just a hint of colour leave it for 10 minutes, but for a deeper colour leave for 20–60 minutes. Bear in mind that it always looks darker when the fabric is wet. Once you're happy, rinse the fabric in cold water and wring it out.

- Now fill the bathtub, sink or bowl with cold water and add a few tablespoons of vinegar (to set the colour). If you're using a larger container such as a bath, add a few more tablespoons. Stir the water and steep the fabric for about 10 minutes. Give it a final rinse and let it dry. Some people say ironing the fabric at this stage also helps to set the colour.

CUSHIONS

Soft furnishings provide the ultimate finishing touch, but they can also be very expensive. However, with a little know-how they can be really easy to make. Once you have chosen your fabric and made your first cushion, I bet you one large velvet pouffe you will never buy off the shelf again.

The trick is not to be intimidated by over-complicated instructions. Instead, find an easy project with simple stitches and just take your time. If you need guidance on basic sewing, you'll find everything you need to know in the sewing section of this book (see pages 24–35), then you can get going on the projects in this chapter. I have even included a cushion that requires no sewing whatsoever (see page 127).

PROJECT

NO-SEW TASSEL CUSHION

This is a great beginner's project as it requires no sewing at all as the two sides of the cover are knotted together to make decorative tassels. This is an ideal technique for making sofa or bed cushions, large floor cushions and cosy cushions for a dog bed. It's adaptable because you use a cushion pad (pillow form) or bed pillow to fill it, or you can make the cushion cover any size you like and simply stuff it with filling.

You can use any fabric for this project, but I recommend fleece as it does not fray, unlike many other fabrics. Fleece doesn't crease much so there's no need for ironing after it has been washed. (You can't remove the inside easily for washing but you can simply pop the whole cushion in the wash when needed.) I haven't found a huge selection of pretty fleece fabrics here in the UK so you may need to shop around. The fabric I used here is from a brilliant US company that sells beautiful, affordable fabrics (see page 264).

YOU WILL NEED

Cushion pad (pillow form) or
    polyester filling
Tape measure
Fleece fabric
Fabric scissors
Pins
Right-angled ruler
Chalk
Masking tape

STEP 1 - MEASURE AND CUT FABRIC

If using a cushion pad (pillow form) as the filling, measure it and jot down length and width. Now work out the measurements needed for the fleece. This will be the cushion length + 30 cm (12 inches) and cushion width + 30 cm (12 inches). You need the extra 30 cm (12 inches) to allow for the thickness of the cushion (5 cm/2 inches) plus another 12.5 cm (5 inches) on each side to allow for the tassels. Cut two pieces of fleece to these dimensions.

Tip: You may find the tassels are too long but you can trim them at the end – it's better to play it safe than make them too short.

STEP 2 - LINE UP FRONT AND BACK

Lay the fabric for the back of the cushion on a flat surface, right side down, then lay the fabric for the front of the pillow on top, right side up and line up the edges. Pin the two pieces together to prevent them moving.

STEP 3 - CUT OUT CORNERS

Using a right-angled ruler, measure squares of fabric from each corner to match the length of the tassels you plan to cut out. So, for 12.5-cm (5-inch) tassels, cut a 12.5 x 12.5-cm (5 x 5-inch) square from each corner. Measure carefully, then cut out the squares from both layers of fleece (if you wish, mark your cutting lines with pins or draw chalk lines). *See pictures: top and middle.*

STEP 4 - CUT TASSELS

Lay a ruler or place masking tape from corner to corner along each side to use as a guide, then measure and mark fabric strips 2.5-cm (1-inch) wide all around four edges. Cut through both layers of fleece to make tassels 12.5 cm (5 inches) long. Remove any pins or brush off any chalk marks. *See picture: opposite bottom.*

STEP 5 - TIE FRONT AND BACK TOGETHER

Working your way around three sides of the cushion cover, tie up the tassels using a balloon knot (a balloon knot is exactly that, the way you tie a balloon). In fact, any knot would work, but a balloon knot just looks nice and tidy. *See picture: top.*

STEP 6 - FINISH OFF

When three sides are tied, insert your cushion pad (pillow form) or pillow into the cover and continue tying the final side. Alternatively, if you plan to stuff the cushion cover with filling, tie together most of the fourth side and stuff when you only have five or so tassels left to go. If you wish, trim the tassels to your chosen length. *See pictures: middle and bottom.*

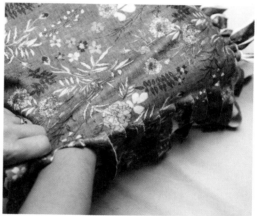

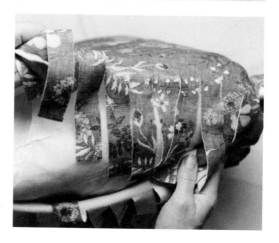

PROJECT

SIMPLE CUSHION

This envelope cushion is the simplest cushion you can make with a sewing machine. My good friend Trish, who is a seamstress extraordinaire, showed me how to make this cushion. It's a lot simpler than the cushion covers I used to make, but since mastering this technique I haven't looked back. You can remove the cushion pad (pillow form) so it's easy to wash, and while you can hand stitch this, I'd recommend using a sewing machine as it will be much quicker, stronger and, above all, more enjoyable to make. If you've never used a sewing machine before, go to page 26 for some gentle encouragement and help on getting started.

YOU WILL NEED

Fabric (see step 1 for dimensions)
Tape measure
Fabric scissors
45 x 45-cm (18 x 18-inch) cushion
    pad (pillow form)
Pins
Iron
Sewing machine and matching thread
Pen

Tip: For this cushion choose a linen-cotton fabric that isn't too thick or thin, and if you are a beginner I'd suggest you pick a fabric with a repeating pattern or design, so you don't have to worry about getting an image perfectly centred on the front of the cushion cover.

STEP 1 - MEASURE FABRIC

These instructions are for a 45 x 45-cm (18 x 18-inch) cushion, so adjust the measurements accordingly if your cushion is a different size. Measure out one long panel of fabric 50 cm (20 inches) wide by 120 cm (48 inches) long – this allows plenty of fabric for the envelope foldover (which is the opening where you pop your cushion in). Cut out the fabric. *See picture: top.*

STEP 2 - HEM FABRIC

Double hem both short ends. To double hem, fold over 1 cm (½ inch) of fabric, pin in place, then press all the way along with your iron. Fold over another 1 cm (½ inch) and press again. Sew along both those hemmed ends using your machine.

STEP 3 - FOLD FABRIC

Place the hemmed fabric right side up. Fold in one third of the fabric to the centre, then fold in the other side until you have a folded piece of fabric measuring 46.25 cm (18½ inches) across from edge to edge. Pin all sides to keep the folded fabric in place. (Note that the envelope opening can be in the centre of the cushion back or to one side, whichever you prefer.) *See pictures: middle and bottom.*

STEP 4 - JOIN SIDES

Measure and draw or pin a line about 2 cm (¾ inch) in on both sides. Sew down both lines, using a double stitch (go forwards, backwards, forwards) over the central join to reinforce. *See pictures: top and middle.*

STEP 5 - NEATEN SEAMS

To keep nice tidy seams, either do a zigzag stitch alongside this seam or do another line of running stitch as I've done. *See picture: bottom.*

STEP 6 - TRIM CORNERS

Finally, snip off the very tips of the corners a little on the diagonal to get a neat corner (this gets rid of bulky fabric in the corners, making a better end result). Iron the cover, then turn right side out and insert the cushion pad (pillow form).
See picture: bottom.

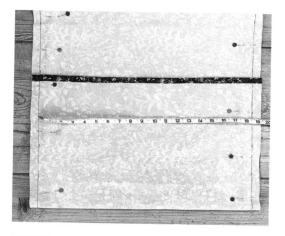

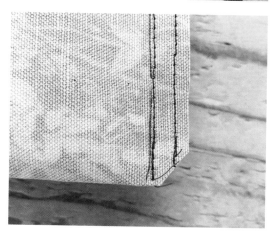

CURTAINS

I seldom buy brand new curtains – not only are they incredibly expensive, but I rarely find new curtains that I like and are in keeping with my cottage style. I do love the soft muted linen curtains that are quite popular nowadays – in fact, I have some hanging in our snug and they look beautiful with sunlight streaming through – but they don't always do the best job of keeping the warmth in. So here are some rather lovely alternatives for dressing your windows.

TABLECLOTH CURTAIN

Allow me to introduce the tablecloth curtain. I own a lot of pretty vintage tablecloths, although I seldom buy them – I just seem to acquire them! They seem to be the kind of thing people collect over time, then find they have no use for so they pass them on to somebody who will appreciate them, and that somebody is usually me.

I don't mind this at all because these cloths really are a thing of beauty, not just visually, but also due to the time, work and detail that have gone into creating them. I wonder what conversations took place as they were being stitched. Were they stitched by a fire in a cottage? Were they made in the workhouse for the gentry? Or in a sewing circle in a fine front room somewhere? We can only wonder. They can be used in so many ways around the house so if you do chance upon a beautiful, reasonably priced tablecloth, regardless of shape or size, just buy it. You will find a use for it one day, and if you don't, you can always gift it to someone who will really love it.

This means I now have a stash of beautiful antique tablecloths in varying shapes and sizes, which I have on show on shelves and in display cabinets until I need a tablecloth, a bridal veil for my four-year-old daughter, a bed cover for her teddy hospital, or a curtain... If truth be told, I currently have more tablecloths and napkins adorning my windows than I do actual curtains, as they are just incredibly versatile and make such beautiful window coverings. (In fact, my wedding dress was made from an antique Normandy lace bedspread, which also served as our living-room curtain for three years prior to our wedding!)

PROJECT

BLANKET AND LACE CURTAIN

This is an excellent no-sew project not only because it looks beautiful and homely, but because it is also extremely insulating, can be made in minutes and only three items are needed to make it. Blankets and lace tablecloths can often be sourced from charity shops, and the pincer clips are available online or in large craft shops. I use this particular curtain to insulate my cottage during the winter months, but the same principle works just as well in warmer weather, when I simply remove the blanket and keep the pretty lace tablecloth hanging through the spring and summer months.

YOU WILL NEED

A plain fleece or woven blanket, big enough to cover the entire doorway or window with no gap at the bottom

A lace tablecloth, similar in size to the blanket

Curtain rings with pincer clips – make sure they are big enough to fit your curtain pole

STEP 1 - POSITION LACE

Lay out the blanket and lay the lace over the blanket. Align the centre of the lace tablecloth with the centre of the blanket along the top edge.

STEP 2 - CLIP TOGETHER

Clip them together at regular intervals along the top using the pincer clips. Start from the centre and work your way out.

STEP 3 - HANG CURTAIN

Pop the curtain rings on your curtain rail. It really is as simple as that, and not a needle and thread in sight.

PROJECT

VINTAGE TABLECLOTH CURTAIN

This uses exactly the same method as the blanket and lace curtain (see page 137), just without the blanket. All you need is your fabric and pincer clips. The fabric can be a tablecloth, a linen napkin, a pretty tea towel (dish towel) or a length of hemmed fabric. Simply clip the pincer clips across the top at regular intervals and hang. If your fabric is too long you can shorten it quite easily by following the instructions below.

YOU WILL NEED

A vintage tablecloth (or linen napkin, tea towel, hemmed fabric)
Curtain rings with pincer clips
Tape measure
Fabric pen (or pencil or chalk)
Iron
Matching needle and thread, or fusible hemming tape
Scissors

STEP 1 - MEASURE CURTAIN DEPTH

Hang your pincer clips on the curtain rail, then measure the distance from where the clip grips the fabric to the bottom of the windowsill. Then add 5 cm (2 inches) to that measurement to allow for hemming.

STEP 2 - CUT FABRIC

Lay out your tablecloth with the wrong side facing up. From the top edge, measure how long you need the curtain to be, and mark it with a dot on the bottom end. Do this at either edge of the fabric, and in the middle. Draw a line all the way across the fabric joining the dots, then cut along that line.

STEP 3 - CREATE DOUBLE HEM

Fold the cut edge over by 2.5 cm (1 inch) and press flat with an iron, then fold it over another 2.5 cm (1 inch) and press again. Sew along the fold using slip stitch (see page 33). Alternatively, for a super quick no-sew fix, place some hemming tape between the folds and press with an iron to fuse. Hang the curtain by clipping the fabric into the pincer clips.

PROJECT

EASY CUPBOARD CURTAIN

Kitchen cupboard curtains are a quintessential feature of a country cottage kitchen. They are also incredibly handy because they hide a multitude of unattractive things. I have used a tablecloth for this project, because it means three of the sides are already finished, and all I have to do is fold over the top and sew in place. I've called this a cupboard curtain, but the same process can be used to make any curtain.

YOU WILL NEED

Tablecloth
Tape measure
Pencil, chalk or fabric pen
Fabric scissors
Pins
Iron
Sewing machine
Curtain wire, hooks and eyes

STEP 1 - MEASURE UP

Measure the space you want this curtain to cover and write down the length and width. You'll need a tablecloth that is roughly double the measured width (to allow for gathering) and at least 6 cm (2⅜ inches) longer than your measured length (to allow enough fabric to make a channel for the wire to pass through along the top).

STEP 2 - CREATE WIRE CHANNEL

Lay the fabric out, right side down, fold over the top by 3 cm (1¼ inches) and press with iron. Now fold over again by another 3 cm (1¼ inches), press with iron again and pin in place.

STEP 3 - STITCH CHANNEL

Machine sew all the way across 5 mm (¼ inch) from the bottom edge of the channel, using running stitch. When you get to the end, reverse for a few stitches, then sew forwards again to finish, then cut the threads. Then repeat this process all the way across 5 mm (¼ inch) from the top edge. This will give a dainty edge along the top and ensure the wire isn't putting pressure on the fabric.

STEP 4 - HANG CURTAIN

Screw the eyes into the walls and the hooks into the ends of the curtain wire. Thread the wire through the channel, gathering the fabric evenly, and hang.

PROJECT

RIBBON-TIE CURTAINS

This project uses a sewing machine, but all you need to know is a basic running stitch. I made one panel here as my window isn't very wide, but you can just as easily make two. To make the process quick and simple, this curtain has ribbon ties along the top, so there is no fiddly business with pelmets, pleats and suchlike.

YOU WILL NEED

Curtain fabric
Curtain lining
Wide ribbon
Tape measure
Right-angled ruler
Pins
Rotary cutter and cutting mat (these are preferable, but scissors would be fine)
Fabric scissors
Fabric pen (or chalk or pencil)
Sewing machine
Needle and thread
Curtain weights (optional)

STEP 1 - MEASURE UP

Measure the width and height of your window and decide on the size you would like your curtains to be. They need to be a fair bit wider than the window (usually at least one and a half times wider) so they look ample and drape well. When you've decided on your measurements, add 10 cm (4 inches) to the height measurement and 18 cm (7 inches) to the width to allow for hemming and edging – these are the measurements for the curtain fabric. Separately list the measurements for the curtain lining as this needs to be 20 cm (8 inches) narrower in width to allow for the 'return'.

STEP 2 - SQUARE UP FABRIC

Before cutting the fabric, ensure you have straight edges on all sides – if you start with a wonky edge, you will have a wonky curtain that does not hang properly. This process is called squaring up. Fold the curtain fabric in half lengthwise, bringing the selvages of the fabric together (the selvage is the self-finished edge of fabric, which keeps the fabric from unravelling or fraying). Align them on a large table or work surface. Keep the selvages carefully together with one hand, but allow them to slide up or down as needed while you smooth the folded fabric with your free hand. When everything is flat and smooth, fasten the selvages together with pins to keep them aligned. Lay a right-angled ruler on the fabric so that one edge lines up with the selvages and the other leg crosses the fabric at a 90-degree angle close to the end. Hold the square firmly and use a rotary cutter on a cutting mat to remove the uneven excess from that end of the fabric (you can use scissors but you'll get a cleaner finish with a rotary cutter). Do the same for the other end to get a perfectly squared-up piece of fabric. Repeat for the lining.

STEP 3 - MEASURE AND CUT FABRIC

Lay your curtain fabric out flat. Using a long ruler measure how long you need the curtain to be, and mark it with a dot. Do this on both sides, then draw a line all the way across the fabric joining the two dots, using a fabric pen that disappears when ironed. Then cut along that line. If needed, repeat this process along one side of the length to get the right width. Next, repeat this process for the curtain lining, remembering to make it 20 cm (8 inches) narrower in width as this creates a 'return' edge (when finished, on the lining side you'll have a nice edging of curtain fabric running down both sides).

STEP 4 - SEW SIDES

Now both pieces are ready. Lay your top curtain fabric on a large surface, right side facing up, then lay your lining on top with the right side facing down. Align the edge of the curtain fabric with the edge of the lining and pin all the way along, then repeat on the other side. Then sew both sides on your machine using a simple running stitch, stopping about 7.5 cm (3 inches) from the bottom. Don't worry that the lining is narrower and doesn't lay flat at this point – that is due to the 'return' and all will become clear soon. *See pictures: top and middle.*

STEP 5 - CREATE RETURN

Now you need to find the centre of both pieces of fabric on the top edge. Do this by taking hold of each corner of the curtain fabric (the top edge), fold it in half and mark the centre point with a dot. Then do the same to the lining fabric. Align those two dots together and pin in place, then smooth the curtain out on a large surface. Now press along the top with the iron from the centre outwards and along both sides and you'll see how this creates the returns along the sides. *See picture: bottom.*

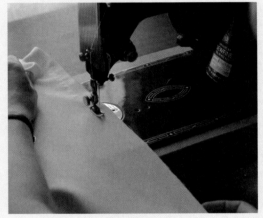

STEP 6 - ADD RIBBON

Now the sides are sewn together, it is time to add the ribbons. Along the top use a fabric pen to mark where you would like the ribbon ties to go, starting from the centre. Make sure they are evenly spaced and that the gaps are not too big, otherwise the fabric will sag. It's also vital to have a tie very close to each end of the curtain so it hangs nicely. When you know how many you need, measure and cut your ribbon. For my curtain I used nine ties in total, so I cut 18 pieces of ribbon, each measuring about 36.25 cm (14½ inches) to allow for the bow. Lay two pieces of ribbon wrong sides together and place them on the inside of the curtain with the top of the ribbon aligned with the top edge of the curtain. Pin all the ribbons in place and machine sew along the top edge of the curtain. *See pictures: top, middle and bottom.*

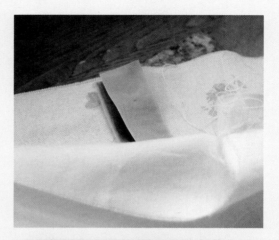

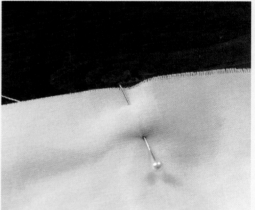

STEP 7 - PRESS CURTAIN

Turn your curtain right side out and give it a good press with the iron. Good curtain making is all about measuring and pressing. Once it is nicely pressed and flat, turn it inside out again and smooth it out.

STEP 8 - HEM CURTAIN

Turn up the bottom edge of the curtain fabric 2.5 cm (1 inch) and press, then do it again and pin all the way along. Then do the same for the lining, except add an extra fold to ensure the lining is hanging 2.5 cm (1 inch) or so above the curtain fabric. If you want to add weights to the bottom, you can do so now – I inserted a small coin when I folded in each corner. Then hand sew both hems separately using whip stitch or slip stitch (see pages 32–33). Don't be tempted to sew the fabric and lining together, as curtains hang much better when the lining and fabric are not joined at the base hem. *See pictures: top and bottom.*

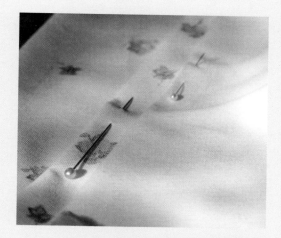

STEP 9 - HANG CURTAIN

Turn the curtain right side out. Feed one ribbon from each pair through each curtain ring, then tie the pair of ribbons in a tight bow. I chose a velvet ribbon – once the ribbons were tied, I trimmed the ends on the diagonal to prevent fraying.

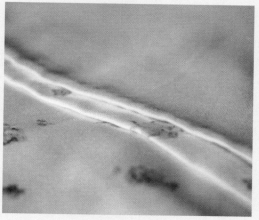

CURTAIN ALTERNATIVES

Sometimes you come across a window that needs some sort of covering, although not necessarily a regular curtain or blind (shade). This may be because of its shape or size, or simply due to the window placement in the room. I have several windows like this in my own house, and I often end up having to think outside the box. To me, a window without any dressing can feel like an eye without an eyebrow! Here are a few examples of how I've dressed tricky windows.

DECORATIVE CURTAINS

This window is next to the fireplace in my living room and looks out onto the garden. I love the view throughout the year, the way the grasses silhouette against the sky and how the bats flit around at dusk. This window frames the scene like a work of art so I wanted to make the most of this feature and dress it beautifully without hanging a blind or curtain to obstruct the view. After trying a few options, I found a simple, delicate piece of lace fabric was just the ticket. It is an old narrow remnant but draped in this way, it works perfectly. I simply screwed two hooks in the top corners of the window recess and draped the fabric across. There is only one window on this wall so I found that framing it on the left side not only softens the edges of the window, but also provides balance on that wall too.

PROJECT

EMBROIDERY HOOP WINDOW SHADE

In our guest bedroom there is a tiny, high window that is much too small to add any kind of curtain. However, although it is small, it lets in a lot of light, which is not ideal if our guests are wanting a long, lazy lie-in. So I needed to find a way to shut out the light without blocking the light during the day, and saw the solution hanging on the back of my craft-room door – an embroidery hoop! Choose one that is slightly bigger than the size of the window and cover it with a pretty fabric (preferably dark if you want to shut out more light).

YOU WILL NEED

Embroidery hoop
Fabric
Fabric scissors

STEP 1 - INSERT FABRIC

This couldn't be easier. Simply separate the two hoops, lay the fabric right side up over the smaller hoop and lay the bigger one back on top and tighten the screw to secure (this will take all of 60 seconds to do).

STEP 2 - TRIM FABRIC

Now trim the excess fabric from around the hoop. Guests can simply lean the fabric-covered hoop against the window at night, then put it to one side in the morning.

PROJECT

FABRIC AND LACE HAND TOWELS

Fabric- and lace-edged guest towels add a lovely finishing touch to a cottage bathroom as well as making gorgeous gifts. If you can sew in a straight line on a sewing machine, then you can do this. Any machine-washable cotton fabric will work for the border. You can create a matching set or opt for a mismatched collection in pretty vintage florals to bring some colour and cottage charm to your bathroom.

YOU WILL NEED

Good-quality plain white towels
Fabric
Fabric pen (or a regular pen
    will suffice)
Lacy ribbon
Fabric scissors
Iron
Pins
Sewing machine and thread

STEP 1 - MEASURE FABRIC

You will need an even strip of fabric to sew onto each towel. To do this, lay your fabric out. Ensure you have one straight edge to begin with, then measure 10 cm (4 inches) down from that edge and mark with a dot. Do this at each end and in the middle – this ensures it's even all the way along. Fold over and press with your iron. *See picture: top.*

STEP 2 - MEASURE TOWEL

Next measure the width of the towel, add 2.5 cm (1 inch) to each end and mark this measurement out onto your fabric, then fold along that line, press and cut. *See picture: middle.*

STEP 3 - FOLD FABRIC

Now fold over about 1.5 cm (5/8 inch) on each edge of the strip and iron flat. *See pictures: bottom, and opposite top.*

STEP 4 - THE FABRIC STRIP

Now you have a tidy strip. You could sew this on as it is, folding the short ends under, or add some ribbon.

STEP 5 - ADD RIBBON

To add ribbon, make sure it measures the width of the towel plus 2.5 cm (1 inch) at each end (for overhang), lay the ribbon onto the fabric and pin in place, ensuring each end is folded neatly under at each end. Then pin the strip to the towel. *See picture: middle.*

STEP 6 - SEW IN PLACE

Sew each edge in place. Start by sewing the ribbon in place, then move onto the edges. You can either leave a 5-mm (¼-inch) gap from each edge or sew quite close to the edge. *See picture: bottom.*

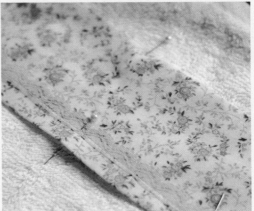

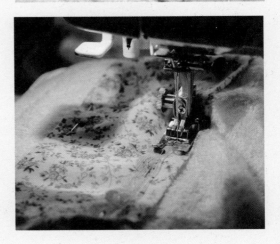

WINTERFYING THE HOME

As I write this, it is November here in England and very chilly. Our dog Ralphy is snoring in his bed, the fire is crackling and I am sitting snuggled under a blanket with a hot cuppa by my side. If Jack Frost is nipping at your heels, it is time to batten down the hatches and 'winterfy' your home. 'Winterfy' isn't a word you'll find in the dictionary but it perfectly sums up 'making a home cosy'. Heating our homes is a costly business, but there is a lot we can also do to keep the cold out.

FLOORS

If, like us, you live in an old house you may find the cold sneaks up through the floorboards, so we use rugs where there are no carpets. Good rugs can be quite expensive to buy new but you can easily pick them up secondhand. If you do this, I highly recommend getting them cleaned as you don't want to bring any pests or dust mites into your home, and cleaning is still likely to be much cheaper than buying brand new. If you have the time and inclination, you could also make your own rag rugs.

WINDOWS AND DOORS

These are the major draught culprits. The most affordable way of keeping the cold out when it comes to windows and doors, aside from double-glazing, is curtains. Thick heavy curtains really do make a world of difference, but they can be incredibly expensive to buy. So I came up with a very quick, easy and affordable solution – see my blanket and lace curtain on page 137.

DRAUGHT EXCLUDER

This is a cheap, easy fix for stopping a draught howling under the door. Simply cut one leg from some old thick tights (pantyhose) or leggings and fill with fine gravel, lentils or rice. Then tie with pretty ribbon at either end.

PROJECT

KEYHOLE COVER HANGER

Sitting at my kitchen table, I couldn't work out where I was feeling a chill from. When I held my hand over the keyhole there was a real gust of cold air coming through. You can buy a keyhole with a cover but if that's not easily done try my super-quick keyhole cover hangers. You can use them year after year and they block the draughts brilliantly. I store them with my winter clothes and bring them out every autumn.

YOU WILL NEED

Fabric – a great way to use up
  remnants
Fabric scissors
Ribbon
Pins
Needle and matching thread
Sewing machine (optional)
Uncooked rice or lentils

STEP 1 - CUT FABRIC

Take two pieces of fabric and cut them both into your chosen shape, adding a hem allowance of 1 cm (½ inch) and choosing a shape and size that will hang comfortably over the keyhole.

STEP 2 - INSERT RIBBON

Lay the first piece face up and pin a folded length of ribbon in place but upside down (so the ends of the ribbon align with the top raw edge of the fabric). Do make sure the ribbon is the right length for your handle – if it's too long it won't cover the keyhole. *See picture: bottom left.*

STEP 3 - PIN TOGETHER

Lay the other piece on top, right side down, and pin around the edge.

STEP 4 - SEW TOGETHER

- To sew by hand: Sew around the edge using back stitch (see page 31), leaving a big enough gap so you can turn it inside out.
- To sew by machine: Sew around the edge using running stitch, leaving a big enough gap so you can turn it inside out. *See picture: bottom right.*

STEP 5 - FINISH OFF

Turn it inside out and fill with uncooked rice or lentils, then hand stitch the gap closed using invisible ladder stitch (see page 35) and secure with a knot at the end.

LIGHTING THE WAY

WHATEVER THE SOURCE,
WHEN IT COMES TO COTTAGE LIGHTING,
AMBIENCE IS EVERYTHING

Lighting is an art in itself. It is about setting the scene and creating an atmosphere that makes you feel good. If it makes you smile, you're on the right track.

While I am by no means an expert when it comes to illumination, I have learned through trial and error what works, and what doesn't work, in my own little abode. Lighting is of course down to personal preference – while spotlights may work a treat in many homes (my husband would happily install spotlights if given the choice), for me, when it comes to cottage lighting, ambience is everything. You can be quite clever with lighting – by highlighting the areas you like, you can draw attention away from areas you are not so keen on, so think carefully about which areas of the room you want lit.

LAMPS

Lamps are my go-to lighting source as they are so versatile. However, where you place them, the bulb you use (see page 164) and the style of lamp can make all the difference. Take into consideration the size of the room – for example, a very small lamp in the corner of a large room with a tall ceiling might look rather silly, and the bulb just won't have the reach. That may seem obvious but it's an easy mistake to make.

If you love rustic cottage style, then using a few different lamps of various heights and styles is a great way to bring interest to a room, rather than using three identical lamps. The colour of the shade can also make a difference, and what looks lovely when the lamp is switched off may not necessarily look good on, and vice versa. While neutral or beige lamps might seem like a safe bet, these may lead to a room looking a little dull if that's all you use, so introducing a slightly warmer colour, such as peach or terracotta, can give a room some depth and a richer, warmer glow. In a nutshell, if you're looking for warmth, use warm colours and steer clear of cool tones such as greys and blues.

MOOD LIGHTING

Strings of fairy lights are not just for Christmas. Used in the right way they can bring character and drama to a room. Battery-operated fairy lights can also be extremely handy for lighting areas where you want some light or ambience but there are no electrical sockets, or it's an awkward space. Fairy lights inside glazed cabinets can be a lovely way to light glassware or curiosities. You can weave them around anything. However, do try them first – some have a lovely warm glow, while others can appear quite cold.

CANDLES AND OLD-STYLE LIGHTS

Candles, gas lamps and hurricane lamps are perfect cottage lights. I picked up our gas lamp many years ago in an antique shop and I just love it, especially now you can buy smokeless, odourless lamp fluid. These lights bring a timeless feel and energy to our little snug on a dark winter's night. You just have to treat the lamp with care and make sure it's in a safe place where it can't be knocked or grabbed by small hands.

Candles are a wonderful source of light and energy in a home. I do have battery-operated candles dotted around so my little one can turn them on by herself, but nothing beats real candlelight. Lighting candles may seem a faff to some, but it can become a special part of your day, a little ritual and moment of calm to mark the end of your working day, before you step into your evening. I highly recommend making my pressed flower tea lights as they look particularly beautiful on a dining table (see page 181). Just remember the usual safety precautions – never leave naked flames unattended and always place out of reach of children and pets.

BULBS

LED bulbs have now replaced the old-style incandescent bulbs and while they are much more cost-efficient, the light they give off just isn't as pleasing. I've scoured the earth looking for LED bulbs I like and a very informative woman at a lightbulb company recently gave me some crucial information on choosing a lightbulb.

Firstly, if you're after a warm white (which is nicer and much more ambient than cool white) always look for a kelvin scale of 2700. Secondly, opt for a filament bulb – this is all glass, instead of half plastic/half glass. Lastly, the information on the bulb packaging can be very confusing, but the number you're looking for is the 'lumens' as this equates to the older style of specifying the wattage of a bulb. So, 100 watt = 1521 lumens, 60 watt = 806 lumens, 40 watts = 470 lumens and 25 watts = 250 lumens.

The vintage-style LEDs may look quite attractive but I find their light is always too warm or yellow. Whatever you buy, do try the bulbs out at home and don't be afraid to ask the shop to change if you're not happy. It doesn't matter how much time, money and effort you have invested in a room, light it badly and it can look as dull as dishwater. I've known people to redecorate their homes because they think they're not happy with the walls, decor and furniture, until eventually it transpires that actually it is their lighting that they don't like.

OUTSIDE LIGHTING

The same thought that goes into lighting our homes can absolutely be applied to the garden, and how we light it can make all the difference. I love to create pockets of interest in our garden – there are strings of fairy lights in trees, lights along paths, lights over my little girl's fairy arch and lanterns dotted in and around the flowerbeds. Thankfully there is so much affordable, solar-powered lighting available now, so it's not hard at all to light up our gardens.

My favourite area is our courtyard, as we have festoon lights draped all around it and they illuminate it so beautifully, whatever the season.

TECHNIQUE

FABRIC LAMPSHADE

Rather than buying brand new ready-made lampshades, it can be cheaper to make your own using a lampshade kit, which also means you can choose your own fabric and make something bespoke. All the lampshades I feature in this chapter are made using a basic kit which contains everything you need except the fabric. The companies that make these kits usually sell the individual components separately too, so you can upcycle old lampshades if you wish. This is especially handy when you have a particular size of lampshade that suits an existing lampstand, for example.

You'll find a huge array of lampshade kits in various shapes and sizes, which can be adapted for lamps or ceiling lights. My instructions should work with most lampshade kits, but do check to make sure they are compatible with your kit. Once you have tried your hand at making one, I guarantee you will be hooked. You'll be making lampshades for every room in the house in no time.

When it comes to choosing fabric for lampshades, try not to opt for anything too thick as it will be hard to work with. Also bear in mind what it will look like with light shining through because if it is too thick, light will not penetrate well. Try holding your fabric up to a light when choosing to see if you like the 'glow'. A plain solid colour or a repeating pattern is probably easier to use as it doesn't matter where you lay your panel. My fabric features a woodland scene so I had to centre the pattern, but if your fabric doesn't require this you can hop to step 2.

YOU WILL NEED

Lampshade kit (this should include the drum lampshade frame, self-adhesive lampshade panel, double-sided tape and a pokey tool)

Fabric
Iron
Pins or invisible fabric pen
Scissors

STEP 1

Cut your fabric to the size specified in the kit instructions. Iron your fabric and lay it out pattern side up. Without peeling the backing from the self-adhesive panel, lay it on top, covering the area you want to use (weigh it down at each end to keep it in place). When you are happy with your placement, put some pins around the panel 2.5 cm (1 inch) from the edge to use as markers, or use an invisible fabric pen.

STEPS 2 & 3

Turn the fabric over so it's right side down, (and with the top edge furthest from you). Start by unpeeling approximately 12.5 cm (5 inches) from the adhesive panel and, working from one end of the fabric, carefully stick it down on the fabric. Press down firmly with your fist.

STEP 4

Slowly remove more of the backing little

by little with one hand, while smoothing it down with the other.

STEPS 5 & 6

Now cut out the panel, keeping as close to each edge as possible. However, to avoid a frayed edge leave an extra 5 mm (¼ inch) at one end and 3 mm (⅛ inch) at each side, which will be folded over at a later stage. (Kit instructions don't usually suggest this, but you do get a more professional finish.)

STEP 7

To remove the scored bendy edges of the self-adhesive panel, bend them back until you hear them crack, then peel them away. When finished, snip off any frays.

STEP 8

Lay a strip of double-sided sticky tape across the plastic end where you left the extra bit of fabric. Peel off.

STEP 9

Fold the fabric back over the tape and stick down firmly.

STEPS 10 & 11

Lay another strip of tape over the top, but don't peel this off yet as we first need to make the lampshade rings sticky. Take one ring at a time, apply a strip of double-sided sticky tape all the way around each ring, wrapping it round the edge as you go. Leave

a tiny gap between strips to allow you to peel off the backing.

STEP 12

Peel the tape backing from each ring. Starting at the opposite end from the end with the line of tape, stand the rings onto the edge of the plastic (make sure it's on the plastic, not on the fabric). Get one in place first, then the other, then slowly start rolling them forward. Keep an eye on the edges as you go to make

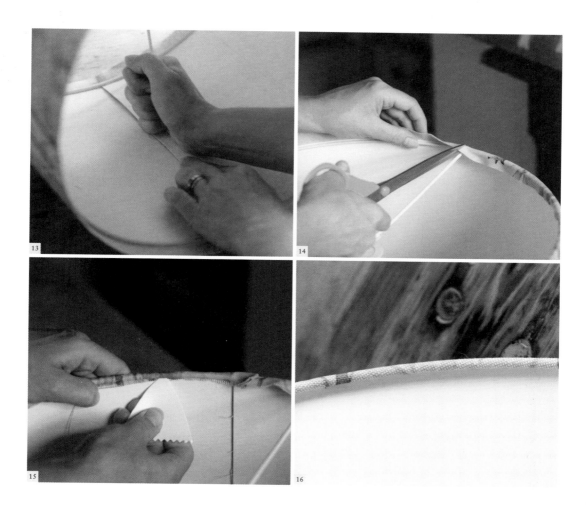

sure everything is straight. When making a ceiling shade, make sure the ring with the light fitting is at the top.

STEP 13

When you get to the end, peel off the sticky tape and press down firmly to seal the two ends of the fabric shade together.

STEP 14

If your lampshade has the cross bars on one of the rings as mine does, make a little snip above each one.

STEPS 15 & 16

Using your hand, fold over the fabric on each edge, then use the pokey tool to push the fabric under the edge of the ring and tuck in any frayed edges. You will need to push quite hard until you hear a click. If the pokey tool bends, simply cut to give a sharper edge.

PROJECT

PRESSED WILDFLOWER LAMPSHADE

Of all the things I've ever made, I think these pressed flower lampshades are my favourite. I have several dotted around my house and they are just so beautiful, on or off. But not only that, it's the joy they have given me from start to finish. I remember the walk where I picked the flowers, I remember making each and every one. But that's the thing about handmade, you're not just making things, you are also making memories along the way. If you haven't pressed flowers before, turn to page 222 for a straightforward guide. For this project you will need very delicate flowers and grasses that are completely dry and pressed well.

I always use lokta tissue paper for this project as it has a lovely natural texture, it's ultra-fine and lightweight but strong, and it moulds beautifully around the flower shapes (see stockists, page 264). If you use a thicker paper, the light won't shine through and the flowers won't stand out. Note that the flowers are placed between the paper and the self-adhesive backing panel.

I highly recommend you give this project a go, but I would suggest you make the simple fabric lampshade on page 167 first, so you can get to grips with the method. The process for this project is exactly the same, but instead of fabric, you cover the lampshade in natural paper. It's just as straightforward but you do need patience, so take your time, breathe and enjoy.

YOU WILL NEED

Lampshade kit (this should include the lampshade frame, self-adhesive lampshade panel, double-sided tape and a pokey tool)

Selection of pressed flowers
Natural lokta tissue paper
Scissors
Pencil or pins

STEP 1 - PREPARE PAPER

Lay your paper out right side down (if using lokta tissue paper, the textured side is the right side). Without peeling the backing from the self-adhesive panel lay it on top of your paper, covering the area you want to use (weigh it down if you need to). Draw a rough outline in faint pencil about 5 cm (2 inches) around the whole outline. This is to mark the approximate perimeter for placing your flowers.

STEP 2 - PLACE FLOWERS

Put the self-adhesive panel to one side and begin laying out your flowers on the paper in a design of your choosing. You can place them all vertically, which looks really lovely on a drum shade, or you can cross and overlap them. Perhaps try a few different ways until you are happy. *See picture: top.*

STEP 3 - REMOVE TOP AND BOTTOM EDGES

Now remove the long scored edges on both top and bottom of the self-adhesive panel. (When making a fabric shade, as on page 169, this is done once it's stuck to the fabric but with paper they have to be removed first.) Unpeel approximately 12.5 cm (5 inches) from the self-adhesive panel and carefully stick it down to one end of the paper, pressing down firmly with your fist.

Note: Refer to the fabric lampshade on pages 168–171, steps 3–16, from here if you'd like to see photos of the following steps.

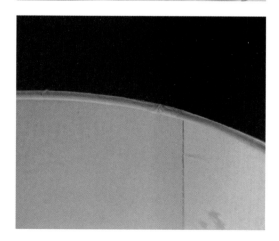

STEP 4 - REMOVE BACKING

Slowly remove more of the backing bit by bit with one hand, while very gently smoothing it down with the other. Take your time and if the flowers move, stop and readjust. If the paper wrinkles on the shade, don't worry as you can smooth that out too. These things add character. If you have another person nearby, you could ask them to hold the paper taut while you do this.

STEP 5 - SMOOTH PAPER

Making sure your hands are clean, flip the panel over and gently run your finger over all the flowers, smoothing the paper into every little crevice. This step really brings out the detail. *See picture: opposite middle.*

STEP 6 - CUT OUT PANEL

To cut the panel out, leave an extra 2.5 cm (1 inch) along the top and bottom and an extra 5 mm (¼ inch) at one end, to fold over and stick down at a later stage.

STEP 7 - APPLY TAPE

Lay a strip of double-sided tape across the plastic end where you left the extra 5 mm (¼ inch). Peel, then fold the paper back over and stick down firmly. Take another line of tape and lay it over the top, but don't peel this off yet.

STEP 8 - PREPARE RINGS

Take one ring at a time and apply a strip of double-sided sticky tape all the way around each ring, wrapping it round the edge as you go. Be careful not to overlap the ends and leave a tiny gap between strips to allow you to peel off the backing.

STEP 9 - ADD RINGS TO SHADE

Peel the tape backing from each ring. Starting at the opposite end from the end with the line of tape, stand the rings on the edge of the plastic (not on the tissue paper) and slowly start rolling them forward, keeping an eye on the edges as you go. If making a ceiling shade, make sure the ring with the light fitting is at the top.

STEP 10 - SNIP AROUND CROSS BARS

Keep going and when you get to the end, peel off the double-sided tape and press down firmly. If your lampshade has the light fitting bars on one of the cylinders as mine does, make a little snip above each one.

STEP 11 - FINISH EDGES

Using your fingers, carefully fold over the edges on each side and tuck in the paper into the edge. You can use the pokey tool to tuck the edge in but do be careful and don't push it all the way if using paper. *See picture: opposite bottom.*

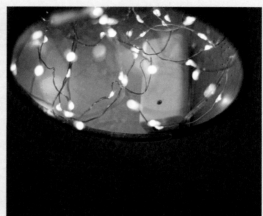

PROJECT

FAIRY LIGHTS LAMPSHADE

This is a great light for a children's room, and as the string of fairy lights is battery operated you can hang and use it anywhere. My little girl sometimes uses this as a nightlight and it regularly lights up her 'den' – wherever that may be. We even use it in the garden during the summer months.

And of course, this project doesn't have to be made for a child. The lampshade would also look beautiful made with pretty floral napkins, which you could hang from trees or anywhere you wanted a little bit of mood lighting. Simply decorate to suit your space or occasion. You can read more about decoupaging with napkins in the Basic Techniques chapter (see pages 46–49).

I chose a small lampshade for this project as I wanted it to be the same size as the image on the napkin, but you can adapt this to a shade of any size. A floral pattern would work well, but bear in mind that if you use a larger lampshade you will see the join so think about how that would look (although a mismatched patchwork style would look good). Whatever you do, lay the napkins out and have a play before you commit.

Follow the instructions for making the fabric lampshade on page 167. Napkins have three layers to them, so remove the middle and back layers, and just use the very top layer with the image on. The string of fairy lights can be popped inside the finished lampshade. I also pricked some holes in the shade to let light through and enhance the overall effect.

PROJECT

NATURE CHANDELIER

This centrepiece is a wonderful way of bringing light and decoration to an indoor or outdoor room. It often hangs in our living room and I love to decorate it to suit the season. In autumn it is covered with a faux (but very realistic) garland with added pine cones and berries, while in spring it looks lovely with ivy wound around it, but it looks just as attractive when completely bare and covered in twinkly lights.

I've used a string of battery-operated fairy lights as it enables me to move it to other areas of the house and garden, but you can just as easily cover the wreath with plug-in fairy lights for a more permanent fixture. I used a 70-cm (28-inch) wreath base of woven twigs but you can choose a shape or size to suit the dimensions of your room.

Simply wrap the string of fairy lights around the wreath and tuck in the ends. To hang the wreath, tie three pieces of brown string, wire or ribbon around the wreath at evenly spaced intervals. If you'd like a more professional-looking hoop, cut the string at the same equal lengths, pop the ends through a small metal hoop and bind with string or wire. If using string, you could apply some glue before binding for added strength. Then decorate however you wish, adding fresh or faux flowers or foliage.

PROJECT

PRESSED FLOWER TEALIGHT HOLDER

This is such a lovely project. My little girl and I made several of these candle holders and the pressed flower port decanter in less than an hour. It's so simple to do, but look how effective they are. She added the glitter of course, which I now rather like. They look so pretty indoors or outdoors, and they would make the perfect wedding table addition. Keep your eyes open for any little glass yogurt pots, dainty jam jars or unusually shaped glass bottles on your travels, as they would all be ideal for this make.

YOU WILL NEED

PVA or Mod Podge glue
Paintbrush
Glass jar
Pressed flowers (see page 222)
Glitter (optional)
Twine or ribbon
Tealight (real or battery-powered)

STEP 1 - ATTACH FLOWERS

Put your glue in a container, add a little water to it and mix. PVA will look less milky when dry if made a little thinner. Paint a small area of the jar with a thin layer of glue, and press a dried flower onto the area. It's best to work in small areas, as the glue can dry very quickly. Repeat these steps, covering as much of the jar as you like with pressed flowers.

STEP 2 - COAT WITH GLUE

Once you have placed all your flowers on the jar, let the glue dry. Then cover the entire jar with another thin layer of glue. This will ensure everything is secure and give the jar an even texture all around. If you'd like to give your lantern some added sparkle you could sprinkle some glitter at this stage.

STEP 3 – ADD TWINE OR RIBBON

Once dry, tie or glue your twine or ribbon around the jar and secure. Pop your tealight inside.

Safety tips: Do make sure your ribbon or twine is not obstructing the top of the candle and keep any fabrics well away from the flame.

PROJECT

TWIG CANDLE HOLDER

This is a lovely project to do with children and it looks beautiful twinkling away on the mantel on a chilly autumn night. It also makes a wonderful gift for nature lovers. Simply embellish to your own taste, with berries and acorns, or beads and buttons.

YOU WILL NEED

Twigs of a similar thickness

Straight-edged glass tumbler or
    candle holder

Pruning shears

Brown string or twine

Acorn, pine cones or berries (I also
    added a toy mushroom)

Epoxy adhesive glue

Tealight

STEP 1 - CUT TWIGS

Hold a twig against the glass to determine how tall you'd like your twigs to be and snip. If you'd like a rustic finish, allow an extra 1 cm (½ inch) above the rim and snip your twigs at different angles. Try to avoid trimming twigs once in place as this may cause them to become unstuck.

STEP 2 - GLUE TWIGS

Apply a line of glue along the length of your twig and hold in place against the glass until the glue sets. Repeat with more twigs, working your way around the glass. Make sure you leave tiny gaps between the twigs as that's where the light will shine through.

STEP 3 - WRAP WITH TWINE

When the glass is covered, wrap some string or twine around the centre several times and tie in a knot, then make a bow at the back. To finish, either poke your berries, pine cones or acorns through the string, or simply glue in place. Pop the tealight inside.

PROJECT

LACE CANDLE LANTERNS

I first made these candle lanterns for our wedding day – they decorated the tables, hung from the trees and gave a beautifully atmospheric, ambient glow. They are very easy to make and you can use them time and time again. I use old jam jars, pasta sauce jars and even a pretty little one with shells embossed on the side that once contained cockles. The wire needs to be neither too thin nor too thick – just make sure it is easy to manipulate and is strong enough to keep its shape. The pliers will secure the wire, and the glue will secure the lace. You can be as individual as you like with your decoration. I love the effect of hessian (burlap) on lace and finished with a pastel ribbon.

YOU WILL NEED

Recycled glass jars
Bendy thin wire
Pliers
Lace, hessian (burlap) and ribbon,
  to decorate
Fabric glue (suitable for use on glass)

STEP 1 - PREPARE WIRE

Cut a very long length of the wire. The exact length will depend how long you want the handle to be. Fold it in half and twist along the whole length.

STEP 2 - ATTACH WIRE

Hold one end of the wire to the rim of the glass, wrap the rest around once and twist to secure with the pliers. Make sure it's a little loose around the rim initially – you'll understand why in a minute.

STEP 3 - MAKE HANDLE

Once secured, make a long loop (which will form the handle) and push the end through the gap in the rim on the opposite side. Once pushed through, cut off any excess wire leaving 2.5 cm (1 inch) or so and bend it up on itself, and twist to secure. You'll need quite a big handle so the flame from the candle doesn't make it too hot!

STEP 4 - DECORATE

Cut your lace or fabric to size and glue it to the jar, then wrap a band of hessian (burlap) around it, followed by a ribbon. Just have fun with the decorating and create something to suit your own style and occasion.

FURNITURE MAKEOVER

FIND SOMETHING OLD AND UNLOVED THAT
CAN BE TRANSFORMED INTO SOMETHING
BEAUTIFUL TO BE ENJOYED FOR YEARS

I have so many pieces of furniture around our home that I've created, refurbished or upcycled over the years and they all mean so much more to me than things I've bought brand new.

So here are some projects to help you get started. If you're a beginner, you could start with something simple like a painted chair (see page 193) or just dive into whatever you fancy. You'll find all the essentials you'll need for each project here with simple step-by-step instructions. If you'd like more tips on sanding, painting, distressing and decoupaging, take a look at the basic techniques chapter on page 21.

QUICK PAINT MAKEOVERS

When it comes to home makeovers we often assume it's going to take a lot of time and money, but this needn't be the case. Choosing just a couple of items to lighten and brighten can make the world of difference to a room, and for small projects like these, all you need is some leftover paint or one sample pot. Windowsills, doors, radiators, chairs, stools, shelves and cabinets are all ideal candidates for a quick spruce up.

When buying sample pots make sure it's suitable for the surface you will be painting. A sample pot of chalk paint would be ideal for painting wood but you'll need eggshell or metal paint for radiators. Good paint is expensive, so consider buying it secondhand – many people sell unused cans of paint and for little projects such as these, secondhand is ideal.

Another way to get the shade and finish of your choice is to use a colour-matching service (see page 98), as you can buy paint in a sample-pot size this way.

When it comes to painting wood, regardless of whether you're using chalk paint or eggshell, there is always a chance that the tannins from the wood could seep through and cause yellowing, so it's worth doing a patch test. You'll find more information on patch testing on page 97.

PROJECT

PAINTED DOORS

Doors are great projects for using up leftover paint. Many homes have simple white doors but adding some colour to them, whether it's a pretty, subtle shade or a vibrant pop of colour, can really bring a corridor to life. I always use eggshell paint on doors and windows as it's hard-wearing, wipeable and not prone to marking.

YOU WILL NEED

Door
Screwdriver
Paint scraper (if needed)
Fine or medium grade sandpaper
Brush or cloth
Masking tape
Primer (if needed)
Leftover eggshell paint – I used
   Farrow & Ball in Drop Cloth
Flat paintbrush

STEP 1 - PREPARE

Remove the door handle and any hinges you don't want painted. Here I took the door off its hinges and laid it over my dressing table to paint.

STEP 2 - SMOOTH SURFACE

Scrape off any lumps or peeling paint with a paint scraper, then go over the surface with sandpaper to remove any ridges, until completely smooth and dust free. Brush or wipe with a cloth.

STEP 3 - APPLY MASKING TAPE

Apply masking tape along any edges you want to protect.

STEP 4 - CHECK IF PRIMER IS NEEDED

Check your paint can and if you do need to apply a primer, give it two coats now, allowing it to dry fully between coats. If no primer is required, move on to step 5.

STEP 5 - PAINT

Give the door two coats of eggshell paint, allowing it to dry fully between coats. With a door like this I like to use long, even strokes in the direction of the wood grain for a smooth finish. If there are any brush marks you want to remove, lightly sand between coats.

STEP 6 - ATTACH HANDLE

As I used eggshell paint, there was no need for a final top coat so allow the door to dry, then screw the door furniture back in place.

PROJECT

FROTTAGE PAINTED CHAIRS

Painted chairs make an excellent sample pot makeover. Whether you're painting them a solid block colour or using a multi-tone colour technique, they just add a wonderful splash of colour to a room. I love the various shades of Annie Sloan chalk paint but when deciding what colours to go with for my kitchen chairs, I couldn't choose! So I painted all of our eight kitchen chairs in completely different colours. To do this I used Annie's 'frottage' technique. This is so much fun to do and the effect is so interesting and textured, plus you can layer up as many colours as you like. So do jump in and give this a go, but be warned – it is addictive and there's a good chance you'll want to use this technique on everything!

I found that one sample pot was sufficient to give one chair two coats and add a frottage layer on two of the other chairs. You can also add a splash of water to the paint which will make it easier to apply, and make it go further.

TWO-TONE TECHNIQUE

As well as using the frottage technique on these chairs, you can also use a two-tone technique. It's very straightforward as you just use two different colours in the painting process. Paint the item with one colour, allow it to dry, then paint it another contrasting colour, and leave to dry. Then you simply sand back some of the top colour to reveal the colour underneath. It can be a strong or subtle effect depending on the colours you use and how much you sand back.

YOU WILL NEED

Wooden chairs

Medium grade sandpaper

Sample pots of chalk paint – I used Annie
  Sloan Chalk Paint in Scandinavian Pink
  for the base colour and in Olive for the
  frottage effect

Round paintbrush

Newspaper

Bowl of water

Mix mat (optional)

Round furniture wax brush

Furniture wax – I used Annie Sloan
  Furniture Wax in clear and dark

Lint-free cloth

STEP 1 - APPLY BASE COLOUR

Give the chair a clean and smooth out any
surface bumps with your sandpaper. Chalk
paint doesn't require a coat of primer, but
see page 97 for advice on doing a patch test.
Paint the chair with the base colour, moving
the brush in quick strokes back and forth
until the piece is covered. Allow it to dry
and give it a second coat in the same colour.
See pictures: top and middle.

STEP 2 - PREPARE NEWSPAPER

Now prepare your newspaper by taking a
page and scrunching it up into a tight ball,
then open it out again and leave to one side.
You'll need a few of these prepared.

STEP 3 - DILUTE SECOND COLOUR

Water down your second colour a little – you
can either pour the paint into a container,
add a splash of water and stir until it has the
consistency of single (light) cream, or you

can use a plastic mix mat (I used Frankie's old plastic placemat). Have a bowl of water handy, then just pop a splodge of paint on the plastic mat with your brush, sprinkle over some water (also using your brush), mix it up and off you go. You might need to experiment to find the right consistency, so starting on the underneath of the chair is a good idea.

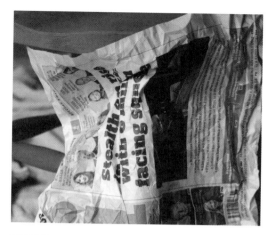

STEP 4 - APPLY SECOND COLOUR

Apply the colour to a section of the chair in the same manner as before. Put the brush down, pick up a piece of newspaper and lay it on top of the wet paint. Smooth it down flat with the palm of your hand (not fingers) and peel it off again to reveal an aged, textured effect. Repeat that process all over the chair with fresh newspaper pages. Don't be too precious about it – you want a variety of uneven effects, with more bits in some places than others. If there's not enough of the second colour showing (if it's too watery and has been absorbed by the newspaper), just add less water. *See pictures: opposite bottom, and here top.*

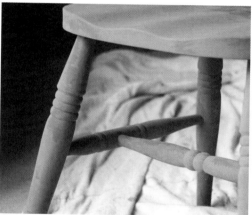

STEP 5 - LEAVE TO DRY

Allow to dry, and if you want to add another colour, repeat step 4 with a third colour. Or if there's something you're not happy with (perhaps there's a really patchy bit), you can go back in now with either of the previous colours and fix it. *See picture: middle.*

STEP 6 - APPLY CLEAR WAX

I waxed some of my chairs with a clear wax, and some with a dark wax to age the further. For tips on waxing see pages 57 and 66. *See picture: bottom.*

PROJECT

DISTRESSED BEDSIDE TABLE

Bedside tables (nightstands) make excellent upcycling projects as they are small pieces and don't take very long to do, especially if you use chalk paint, which doesn't require sanding or priming. Our bedroom is decorated in muted, serene colours and I wanted these drawers to blend in with the overall colour scheme rather than stand out. Swapping the plain wooden drawer knobs for pretty ceramic ones was the perfect way to add a little glamour and femininity to the room. You could use three knobs in the same style or you could opt for three contrasting ones for a quirky alternative (just make sure they are roughly the same size). After my little girl saw this transformation, she insisted she wanted her bedside table redecorated too (although her choice is pink with flower fairies!).

YOU WILL NEED

Bedside table or nightstand
Sandpaper
Furniture chalk paint – I used
    Rust-Oleum Chalky Finish Furniture
    Paint in Hessian
Paintbrush
Clear furniture wax – I used clear
    Briwax
Round wax brush
Lint-free cloth
Ceramic knobs

STEP 1 - PREPARE

Remove the drawer knobs (although if you'd like to paint the existing knobs, you could leave them in place).

STEP 2 - SAND

If your paint surface is uneven, give it a light sanding to smooth out any bumps and then a good brush down. If it doesn't need sanding, go to step 3.

STEP 3 - PAINT

As we're using chalk paint we don't need a primer, so give the drawers two coats of paint, back and forth in all different directions. Allow it to dry in between each coat.

STEP 4 - WAX

You can distress furniture before or after waxing. There is less mess after waxing and you have a bit more control over how much paint you take off too, so that's what I did. Give the furniture a thin, even coat of wax all over either using a round brush or a cloth. Wipe off any excess wax at the end. Allow it to dry for 24 hours.

STEP 5 - DISTRESS

Once the wax is dry, you can distress it. Starting with the main edges, begin running sandpaper back and forth along the edges, until you begin to wear the paint away and you have the desired effect. Pick out any interesting or ornate details, too. See pages 65–67 for more tips on distressing.

STEP 6 - SEAL

If you are happy with a matt finish, leave the piece as it is, going over the distressed areas with a little wax to seal it, then allow it to dry. If you'd like the drawers to have a sheen, you can buff them to a shine with a cloth once dry. Screw the drawer knobs into place to complete the transformation.

PROJECT

OLD WRITING DESK MAKEOVER

I love antiques in their natural state but the transformation of my old writing bureau (she is nicknamed Beatrix!) has really lightened up our living space. For this project I used two different shades of eggshell furniture paint – light grey and white – as I find using two contrasting colours works really well when upcycling furniture. I also decoupaged some of the inside panels using a floral wallpaper, but pages from magazines or even old letters would also look lovely. Just make sure you choose something you love, so it will always bring you pleasure when you sit to write.

YOU WILL NEED

Writing bureau
Fine or medium grade sandpaper
Primer (optional)
Paintbrushes
Furniture paint in two shades – I used
  Laura Ashley paint in Dove Grey
  and Cotton White
Furniture wax – I used Briwax

Lint-free cloth
Wallpaper – I used Laura Ashley
  wallpapers
Scissors
Scrap paper or newspaper (optional)
Mod Podge glue, in matt finish
Polyvine Acrylic Decorator's Varnish
  in clear dead flat finish

STEP 1 - PREPARE

Remove all hinges and knobs, then lightly sand the furniture to remove any lumps and bumps and give it a good brush down. *See pictures: top and middle.*

STEP 2 - APPLY PRIMER

If necessary, apply a coat of primer. Check the labelling on your paint can as some paints (such as chalk paint) do not require priming. If using eggshell pint, a primer will help the paint stick and reduce marks and scratches. Once dry, give it a light sanding and repeat if necessary.

STEP 3 - PAINT FIRST COLOUR

Apply two coats of your first colour everywhere apart from areas that will be covered by the wallpaper. Leave to dry fully between coats, then give it a light sanding.

STEP 4 - ADD SECOND COLOUR

Now it's time for the top colour. I put two coats of the top colour on the front and sides, leaving the inside in the first contrasting colour. I also gave the hinges two coats of white at this point too. Leave to dry fully between coats.

STEP 5 - DISTRESS

Once the paint is completely dry you can distress the furniture (and all hinges and knobs) using fine or medium sandpaper. Start distressing the main edges and corners first, then pick out any detail. I found rubbing lightly but evenly over the embossed drawer with fine sandpaper really brought out the pattern. See pages 65–67 for more tips on distressing. *See picture: bottom.*

STEP 6 - WAX

Give the piece a good dust down and apply your wax with a soft lint-free cloth. Rub it into the grain, then once dry, give it a good buff.

STEP 7 - CUT DECOUPAGE PAPER

Now you can decoupage your paper to the inside. Start by measuring and cutting your paper to size. If you want to play it safe, you could use scrap paper or newspaper to make a template before cutting into the wallpaper. *See picture: top.*

STEP 8 - DECOUPAGE

Apply a thin layer of slightly watered-down Mod Podge glue directly onto the furniture and line up the edge of the wallpaper, gradually laying it down. Smooth the paper out with a clean dry cloth from the centre outwards, removing any bubbles as you go by pushing them towards the edge, and allow to dry. *See picture: middle.*

STEP 9 - FINISHING TOUCHES

To finish, either add a coat of Mod Podge glue on top of the wallpaper, or apply two coats of clear quick-drying Polyvine Acrylic Decorator's Varnish for a durable finish. *See picture: bottom.*

PROJECT

WALLPAPERED CORNER CABINET

My old corner cabinet was another ideal candidate for a spruce up. I first upcycled this many years ago but it was ready for another makeover. The corner of this room is very dark and there are no electric sockets for lighting, so as well as brightening up the cabinet I also added a string of battery-operated fairy lights to the inside. It now looks so pretty in the evenings, and brings an otherwise dull corner to life.

YOU WILL NEED

Corner cabinet
Masking tape
Furniture paint – I used Laura Ashley
   eggshell paint in Cotton White
Primer (if necessary)
Fine grade sandpaper
Putty knife (optional)
Lint-free cloth
Paintbrush
Furniture wax – I used Briwax
Tape measure
Scissors
Wallpaper – I used Laura Ashley
   wallpapers
PVA glue, in matt finish
Brayer or plastic ruler (optional)
Mod Podge or Polyvine Acrylic
   Decorator's Varnish in
   clear dead flat finish
String of fairy lights (optional)

STEP 1 - PREPARE

Remove all hinges and door knobs. You could cover them with masking tape and work around them, but you'll get a much better finish if you remove them. Sand the furniture lightly and give it a good brush down. You don't have to strip it completely, just sand it a little to help the paint stick. *See pictures: top and middle.*

STEP 2 - APPLY PRIMER

If necessary, apply a coat of primer. Check your paint can as some paints (such as chalk paint) do not require priming. If using eggshell paint, a primer will help the paint stick and reduce marks and scratches. If you are transforming something pale, you may only need one coat of primer, but my cabinet was very dark and needed two. Once the first coat is dry, give it a very light sanding, then apply the next one. If you plan to paint your hinges and door knobs, give them a coat of primer too. *See picture: bottom.*

STEP 3 - PAINT

Once the primer is dry, apply your first top coat. Once dry, give it a very light sanding and dust it down, then apply the second coat (and a third if necessary). If you plan to paint your hinges and door knobs, give them a coat of paint now, too.

STEP 4 - DISTRESS

Once the paint is completely dry, it's time to distress. You can use sandpaper alone or use a putty knife as well. If you are painting and distressing your door knobs, you can distress them now. See pages 65–67 for more tips on distressing.

STEP 5 - WAX

Once you've finished distressing, apply the wax with a soft lint- free cloth. You could use a dark wax to give an aged effect, but I wanted to leave this piece looking quite fresh so I used clear. Rub it into the grain, then once dry, give it a good buff. *See picture: top.*

STEP 6 - CUT WALLPAPER

To wallpaper the inside, measure the width and length you need to cover, then make sure your wallpaper edge is straight to begin with. Measure your wallpaper and put a mark on each edge where it needs to be cut, then fold the edge making sure it's straight, and cut to size. Check the wallpaper fits and make any necessary adjustments.

STEP 7 - APPLY WALLPAPER

Apply your first coat of PVA glue onto the furniture. It can dry quickly so ideally have someone to help you – one person can hold the bottom corners while the other can line up the top edge, then gradually lay it down. Once the paper is in place, take a clean, dry cloth and smooth the paper down from the centre outwards, removing any bubbles. A brayer or plastic ruler can help. Some bubbles will disappear overnight; you won't notice any that remain. *See picture: middle.*

STEP 8 - VARNISH

Once the wallpaper is in place and dry, give it a final coat of either Mod Podge or Polyvine Acrylic Decorator's Varnish.

STEP 9 - FINISHING OFF

Once completely dry, screw all hinges and knobs back in place. Add the fairy lights to complete the cabinet. *See picture: bottom.*

PROJECT

FLORAL FARMHOUSE WELSH DRESSER

Stripped-back, bare wood can be a beautiful thing, and in most instances this is my preferred finish. However, some pieces can be vastly improved when painted, such as this Welsh dresser (hutch). I bought this from a charity shop because I liked the shape and detail in the carvings. It had a lot of character but it was very dark and uninspiring, making it the ideal candidate for a transformation with paint and decoupage.

YOU WILL NEED

Welsh dresser
Handheld sander
Masking tape
Fine to medium grade sandpaper
Furniture chalk paint – I used
    Rust-Oleum Chalky Finish Furniture
    Paint in Hessian
Paintbrushes

Floral napkins
Mod Podge or PVA glue
Clingfilm (plastic wrap)
Furniture wax – I used Rust-Oleum
    finishing wax (clear)
Lint-free cloth
Clear matt varnish or Polyvine Acrylic
    Decorator's Varnish

STEP 1 - PREPARE

Remove all screws, hinges and door pulls (I put mine into little cups to keep them organised). *See picture.*

STEP 2 - SAND

Using your sander, take off the top layer of paint or varnish from the areas you want to decoupage. You needn't strip the rest of the piece as you can paint directly on top if your paint allows. Once sanded, give it a good brush down. *See picture: top.*

STEP 3 - PAINT

Apply masking tape to the edges of the areas you plan to decoupage or want to protect – this will ensure sharp, clean edges once removed. Do not paint on the areas you intend to decoupage. Apply two coats of paint to the furniture, sanding in between coats (by hand, not with the sander). Leave to dry and remove the masking tape. *See picture: middle.*

STEP 3 - DECOUPAGE

Separate the very top layer from each napkin so you are left with just the top patterned layer. Most napkins have three layers – peeling the bottom layer off is easy, the second one not so much, so persevere. *See picture: bottom.*

STEP 4 - GLUE

Using a paintbrush, spread an even layer of glue as big as the piece of tissue you're laying. Gently lay the top layer of napkin onto the glue. Then rather than smoothing it down with the brush or your hand, lay a piece of clingfilm (plastic wrap) over it, then smooth the napkin through that with your hand. This stops the tissue from tearing. *See picture: opposite, top.*

STEP 5 - COMPLETE DECOUPAGE

Peel the clingfilm off and very gently apply another layer of glue over the top of the napkin. There will be a few wrinkles, but this all adds to the faded look. If the napkins tear (which mine did), simply tear another piece of napkin the size of the hole you've made and apply it – it won't show once it's dry and sanded. Once all the pieces are in place, leave it to dry.

STEP 6 - SAND

Once completely dry, begin sanding. Using a fine to medium sandpaper, begin gliding the handheld sander lightly over the decoupaged areas, working section by section. This will remove all the wrinkles and leave the surface completely smooth. *See picture: middle.*

STEP 7 - DISTRESS

Once you've sanded the decoupaged areas, brush them down and begin distressing the edges of the furniture using sandpaper. Simply run it over the edges, corners and over any detailing. Brush the furniture down again to remove all dust.

STEP 8 - VARNISH

Give the decoupaged areas a couple of coats of clear matt varnish, allowing it to dry between each coat. This will protect it for years to come. *See picture: bottom.*

STEP 9 - WAX

Apply a thin layer of clear furniture wax to the rest of the woodwork, rubbing it into the grain with a soft cloth, then once dry, give it a good buff or if you want the piece to have a more durable finish, use a clear matt varnish instead.

PROJECT

VINTAGE CRATE SIDEBOARD

This easy project is ideal if you're looking to create extra storage. I was trying to find a home for our ever-growing record collection. I had them stacked in the corner in vintage crates which fitted them perfectly, but thought how nice it would be to have the turntable on top. I had seen tables with hairpin legs and thought that just might be the solution. So I simply joined the two crates together by screwing them to three battens of wood, and then screwed the legs on.

YOU WILL NEED

Vintage storage crates or similar
Battens, planks or scaffold boards,
  cut to size
Sandpaper
Drill
Screwdriver
Screws
4 hairpin legs

STEP 1 - CUT BATTENS

Cut the wood battens to size. If you are not able to do this yourself, you'll find that many hardware shops will be happy to cut them to your measurements. The battens need to be a little shorter than the length of both crates. You can either leave the ends flat or cut them at an angle as here. Once cut, give the ends a good sanding.

STEP 2 - DRILL PILOT HOLES

If you try to screw the battens directly to the crate you run the risk of splitting the wood, so it's a good idea to drill pilot holes first. First drill a small hole, slightly smaller than the screw you intend to use. This will allow your screw to enter into the wood more easily. You might get away without pilot holes when screwing into softwood. Drill the pilot holes in the ends of each batten and screw them onto the crates. To further reinforce, you can then screw the crates together from the inside.

STEP 3 - ATTACH LEGS

When the crates are firmly fixed together, screw the legs to the four corners. Make sure the hairpins all face in the correct direction.

CURIOSITIES

A BEAUTIFUL HOME IS AS MUCH ABOUT SURROUNDING
YOURSELF WITH THE MEMORIES YOU'VE MADE
AS IT IS ABOUT INTERIOR DESIGN

It's sometimes the little things that can make a big difference when it comes to making a house a home, so this chapter is all about those final touches. We'll look at curiosities, and how we can display the trinkets we collect on our travels. We'll embrace nature, finding ways to bring plants and seasonal flowers into our homes, plus wreath making and pressed-flower artwork.

DISPLAYING CURIOSITIES

Whether it's a treasure from an antique shop, a collection of pebbles or a ticket stub from a show you went to in your youth, these mementoes are all captured moments in time. Many homes are filled with such objects, each carrying some meaning or with a memory attached. When I visit a home, it's often these things that I'm drawn to. They tell a story about the people who live there, and they make that house a home.

If you are a minimalist, you may find yourself having slight palpitations at the prospect of a home filled with knick-knacks, but creating an area that you can devote to these meaningful finds is not the same as collecting clutter. A beautiful home is as much about surrounding yourself with the memories you've made as it is about interior design, and those memories deserve their own space.

Quite often we end up stashing old memorabilia. There isn't always a suitable place to put it, and it's not the easiest of things to display. The odd thing on a shelf might look a bit like you've just emptied your pockets. But fill an entire corner cabinet or a whole shelf with these treasures and they can become an artwork, a beautiful piece of your history in their own right.

So have a rummage through your own keepsakes and see what you find, because I guarantee they are likely to be far more fascinating than anything you will find in the shops. Visitors to your home will enjoy seeing these things too, but don't let that be your motivation – this is so you can enjoy and celebrate parts of your own history, as much as your present and future.

DEDICATED SHELVES

I have a few displays of this nature in our house. Upstairs there is a shelf that is dedicated more to the past. You might think you've wandered into Miss Havisham's boudoir as it holds my dried wedding bouquet and the pretty vintage shoes I wore on my wedding day, while our wedding invitation sits next to a photograph of us, snapped in a private moment. Nearby is a pair of red shoes given to me by my late cousin Rita – she told me they once belonged to a woman named Mabel, who loved to dance. She was either jilted or became ill and took to her bed – I can't quite remember as the story has faded in my mind, but I felt that Mabel and her shoes deserve to be remembered. There are other keepsakes too – things we have been given, things that were made for us, and they all have great meaning.

Making such a shelf or cabinet look good is all about trial and error. I'm no interior designer, I just try different arrangements and swap things about until it feels right to me. Take your time, starting with the bigger items. It's about balance, so with a shelf you could try spacing out the larger treasures first, then filling in the spaces around them with smaller items, giving the display some varied height here and there. Point things in different directions so not everything faces the front like ducks in a row. If everything you have is the same height, you could introduce some variation by standing a few things on a plinth, such as a small block of wood. Slide pictures or postcards into the back, too.

CORNER CABINETS

Corners of the room are often dead spaces and a corner cabinet takes up such little room, but holds an awful lot. I keep adhesive tack nearby so I can easily pop postcards and photos on the inside walls of the cabinet, along with the cards from restaurants we've loved or ticket stubs to shows we enjoyed. Then it's a mixture of things from the past and present – photos, an embroidered pincushion, spools of thread. There is a little leaflet box with pamphlets of all the great days out in our area – the kind of thing you would find in a holiday cottage, but why shouldn't we enjoy our home and our surrounding area in the same way? Things like this make it a really joyful, positive corner of the room.

When it comes to arranging your memorabilia in a corner cabinet, try putting the biggest, tallest object in the centre towards the back, then fill in around them. As with shelves, having items facing various directions will help it to look natural. Above all, enjoy this process and everything will soon find its place.

PLANTS

Plants and flowers make a glorious addition to any room, connecting us to nature and bringing greenery and vitality into our space. There are many health benefits to having them nearby, too, including purifying the air.

It's not always easy keeping them alive. I confess some haven't survived under my care for one reason or another, yet others have been with me for years. So if you too have fatally wounded a few plants, please don't write yourself off as a plant killer, just try again. For plants to thrive they like to be in the right position, they need water and some, not all, need plant food. Get those things right and they should flourish for you.

DISPLAYING PLANTS

I have plants dotted throughout most of the rooms in our house. They drape over bookshelves, perch on cupboards and fill any available corner that isn't next to a radiator. Here are a few tips and ideas on where and how to display plants.

SOFTENING AND FILLING EMPTY CORNERS. Having a large plant or mini tree in a corner is a great way to fill and soften the space. If you don't want to buy an enormous ceramic plant pot for the plant to go in, a big straw or rattan basket would be a great, if not better alternative (just remember to place a saucer under the plant pot to catch the water).

DOTTED ALONG SHELVES. Plants on shelves always look pretty, especially trailing plants. Dot them among books and hard objects to help soften the hard lines and add some much-needed yin to the yang.

A PLANT TABLE. While plants look fabulous spaced around the room, they can also look very effective when displayed as an entire collection, either on one table, placed near a window or perhaps on a mini ladder so they're viewed at various heights.

SUSPENDED FROM THE RAFTERS. If you're struggling to find space for plants, get them off the ground and have them hanging from the ceiling instead. They can add interest to a room, and trailing plants especially look wonderful in rope plant hangers (try the super-easy project on page 227).

HANGING FROM THE WALLS. I have a pretty trailing String of Hearts (*Ceropegia woodii*) sitting on an antique sconce on my fireplace wall, and

I love the interest it adds to an otherwise plain wall. Plant or candle sconces are ideal for this purpose, but there's nothing to stop you using a small outdoor pot holder or wall planter inside.

LOW-MAINTENANCE PLANTS. If you love plants but don't want the hassle of watering lots of them, the solution is to get just a few large plants, rather than lots of little ones. They make a great statement and really fill up the space, and it won't take much time at all to care for them.

ARTIFICIAL PLANTS. If you love plants but you either can't have or don't want real plants, you can always cheat. The quality of artificial plants has come on in leaps and bounds. They're especially useful in a windowless room. Fake garlands are ideal for winding strings of fairy lights around and hanging at Christmas. I've put a few lit garlands in Frankie's bedroom and one lights up her play area under the stairs (see page 88).

FLOWERS

Bringing freshly picked flowers into the home is a really easy way of connecting to nature and moving in time with the seasons.

Flowers can bring the most uninspiring rooms to life. If we have friends to stay, I'll always have some little vases of fresh flowers dotted around. We don't need to have enormous flower arrangements on display to make an impact. A small jug or pitcher on the kitchen table, one or two stems in little glass jars on the bathroom windowsill or even a sprig of dried flowers on the bedside table will suffice. Here are some tips and ideas on displaying flowers.

BUY SUITABLY SIZED VESSELS. A giant vase might work in a very large room but would look rather disproportionate in a cosy kitchen. You'd also need to source a huge bouquet of flowers to fill it so when buying jugs, pitchers and vases, be mindful of where the vessel is going. I've always loved collecting vases from charity shops. I'll fill them with dried flowers and grasses through the autumn and winter months, and throughout the spring and summer months, I'll pop in handpicked blooms from the garden. Little antique medicine bottles make lovely holders for single stems, too.

MAKE YOUR OWN VASES. You don't need to buy vases to display flowers – you can just as easily make them. The lace candle lanterns on page 185 work perfectly for displaying flowers. I've put flowers in these jars on many occasions, including my wedding day.

MAKE YOUR FLOWERS GO FURTHER. By using smaller vessels, you will probably be able to fill three or four small vases using only one bunch of flowers. Many flowers have quite a few stems branching off from the main stem, so have a browse at your local florist and choose a selection of bushy multi-stemmed flowers, and you'll find they can go a really long way.

GROW YOUR OWN. If you're lucky enough to have a garden that you can plant in, why not grow your own selection of flowers to cut? It's such a pleasure to pick your own blooms. It will save you money throughout the year, it's better for the environment and you'll be enticing the bees and butterflies into your garden.

DRY GRASSES AND FLOWERS. During the summer months there are beautiful long frothy grasses peppering our hedgerows. I pick a handful of these every year; some I press and others are left in old stoneware pitchers to dry out. Many flowers dry beautifully and it's a great way of having flowers on display if you don't have the time or budget to source fresh ones.

HOW TO PRESS FLOWERS

I absolutely loved pressing flowers with my mum when I was a little girl. So it brings me so much happiness to see my own daughter just as absorbed in the task as I was. She also loves to make flower perfume too, which of course I then have to use!

My flower press is usually full to the brim, so I often press them in heavy books, too – I've often taken a book down from the shelf to read, only to be covered in pressed leaves and petals moments later. I see flower presses all the time in charity shops and they are affordable to buy new too, but there is nothing wrong with using books.

CHOOSING THE FLOWERS

When it comes to pressing flowers, the daintier the flower the better it will press. Bigger, chunkier flowers refuse to squish completely flat. Some will flatten, and might work well on the front of a card, say, but they wouldn't work well in a frame or for use in decoupage. So I suggest choosing flowers with thinner stalks and smaller seedheads, but you'll soon figure this out so don't be afraid to experiment. Some of my favourite plants and flowers to press are love-in-a-mist (*Nigella*), forget-me-nots (*Myosotis*), ferns and the beautiful dainty grasses found in the hedgerows in summertime.

PRESSING THE FLOWERS

Make sure your flowers are completely clean and dry, so picking on a dry day is ideal.

Whether you are using a press or a book, always lay your flowers between sheets of absorbent paper, as this helps to soak up any remaining moisture. Space them out face down. Remember that how you lay your flowers is how they will be preserved.

If you are using a secondhand press you may need to replace the absorbent paper. Then you simply layer the flowers – paper, layer of flowers, paper, layer of flowers, and so on – then finish with a layer of paper and screw on the top of the flower press.

Some people suggest changing the paper every five days. This is only really necessary if the flowers have a lot of moisture in them as this can cause the flower to turn brown. To be honest, I never bother as most of the flowers I press are light and dainty. If pressing thicker flowers such as rose petals, it's probably worth checking them.

PROJECT

PRESSED WILDFLOWERS IN FRAMES

This is a wonderful way to display pressed flowers. Thin, dainty flowers, grasses and leaves work best sandwiched in these double-sided glass frames (if you use something thicker the frame won't close). Flower frames make beautiful gifts, and this is a lovely way of displaying wedding or special-occasion flowers too. Frankie got involved with me here as it's a fun, easy craft to do with children. I used quite a few flowers in my frame, but it needn't be fussy – a single flower can look really effective.

YOU WILL NEED

Double-sided glass frame
Hanging ribbon
Selection of pressed and dried
  wildflowers (see page 222)
Sheet of paper or piece of board, the
  same size as your frame
Tweezers (optional)
PVA glue
Thin paintbrush

STEP 1 - PREPARE FRAME

Clean your glass frame well and make sure it's completely dry. Attach a hanging ribbon that will complement the colour of your flowers.

STEP 2 - ARRANGE FLOWERS

Lay your flowers out on a piece of paper or board, then play around with your design, but work carefully as they're likely to be very delicate.

You may find it easier to move them using tweezers. There is no right or wrong way when it comes to your design – you could arrange them in a straight line or opt for a more natural approach. If you want a natural look try arranging them as you might see them in the wild, for example some of the same flowers might be grouped together, overlapping here and there.

STEP 3 - MOVE FLOWERS TO GLASS

Once you're happy, apply a tiny dot of glue to a couple of places on the back of each flower (with a thin paintbrush, a chopstick or cotton bud/swab) and begin placing the flowers on the glass. I like to start with the biggest flowers.

STEP 4 - LEAVE TO DRY

Leave it to dry completely. Then close your frame and enjoy your artwork.

PROJECT

SIMPLE MACRAMÉ PLANT HANGER

When looking at macramé plant hangers I was taken aback by how much they often cost, so I investigated how they were made. Some are very fiddly and intricate, but to create a simple-but-very-pretty hanger such as this takes all of 15 minutes, and it is very easy indeed. I've added a few wooden beads to mine but feel free to go sparkly or beadless if you wish. Also, do not be put off by the written instructions over the page – they may sound complicated when you read them, but the step-by-step images make it much easier to follow.

My pot was small and light so string worked perfectly fine. If you're planning on hanging a larger, heavier pot, use a thin rope instead, as it's much stronger and will take the weight.

YOU WILL NEED

String
Tape measure
Scissors
Beads (optional)
Screw hook
A plant in a pot

STEP 1 - CUT STRING

Cut five long lengths of string, each measuring 1.5 m (60 inches). If you are making a hanger for a bigger pot, measure 1.8 m (72 inches). *See picture: top.*

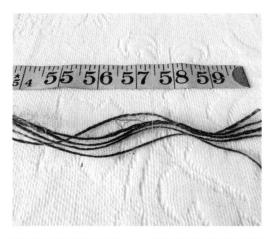

STEP 2 - MAKE LOOP

Line up the five pieces together and find the middle point by folding them in half. Make a loop and tie a knot. The following steps are then much easier because you can hook your loop to something while you knot. So now you will have 10 lengths of string. *See picture: middle.*

STEP 3 - DIVIDE STRING

Divide the 10 lengths of string into five groups of two. *See picture: bottom.*

STEP 4 - FIRST ROW OF KNOTS

Measure 25 cm (10 inches) along on each pair of strings and tie a knot. If you're using beads, thread the bead on before you tie the knot. (In case you're wondering, I didn't put beads on every knot because I only had a total of nine available!)

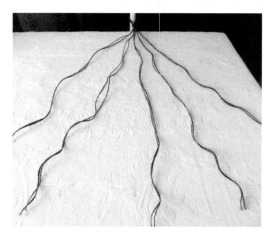

STEP 5 - SECOND ROW

Then, leaving the first piece of string to one side, take the second piece and tie it to the next piece along, leaving a 7.5-cm (3-inch) gap from the knot above. Repeat until you reach the other side. This should leave one remaining piece of string on the far right side. *See picture: top.*

STEP 6 - COMPLETE CIRCLE

Now pick up the two remaining outside pieces of string and join them in the same way, to complete the circle!

STEP 7 - REPEAT KNOTTING

Now repeat the same process on the next row. You can repeat this for as many rows as you like, but as mine is only a small pot so two sufficed. When you get to the end of the row, again join the two outside pieces to form the circle. *See picture: middle.*

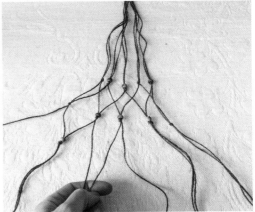

STEP 8 - THE FINAL KNOT

When you've finished your rows, gather all the pieces together (as you would a ponytail) and leaving 7.5 cm (3 inches) from the last row of knots, tie one final knot to bind them all together. Now carefully place your pot inside, fix your hook into the ceiling securely and hang. *See picture: bottom.*

Note: Make sure the hanger and screw can take the weight of your plant, and always make sure the hooks are screwed into the ceiling securely. Screwing the hook into solid wood, such as a wooden beam, rafter or ceiling drywall is ideal. You could use a stud finder to detect a solid wood stud.

PROJECT

VINTAGE MATCHBOX TIN

I bought this lovely little tin from a vintage flea market in Amsterdam many years ago. I often acquire objects without knowing what I'm going to do with them, but I still buy them because I always find the perfect home, or the right job for them, eventually. I was as pleased as punch with myself when I thought of turning this little tin into a working matchbox, because it suits the purpose perfectly and it takes just five minutes to make.

This has now been sitting on my mantel looking pretty and lighting candles and fires for many years. Keep an eye out in antique shops and vintage markets for tins like these, because as well as making one for yourself, they also make the most gorgeous gifts for friends who love their candles.

YOU WILL NEED

An old tin
A large box of matches
Scissors
Double-sided sticky tape

Caution: Do not apply striking strips to the inside of the tin as that would be a fire hazard.

Cut the striking strips from the matchbox, stick on a strip of double-sided sticky tape and apply to the bottom of the tin. When the match-striking paper becomes less effective over time, simply peel it off and replace with new when you refill the box with matches.

PROJECT

TEA STORAGE CADDY

Like many Brits, it is not blood I have running through my veins, it is tea. In our house we get through a variety of different teas throughout the day, my favourite being spiced chai, with 'builders' brew' (aka strong breakfast tea) a close runner up. My husband loves peppermint tea and I'll often finish the day with chamomile. If, like me, you have boxes of tea spilling out from your cupboards, this tea organiser will be just the ticket. Not only does it look dandy on the kitchen worktop but it also frees up cupboard space. The great thing about using metal label holders is you can swap and change the labels easily, so you can use this little chest for tidying away other small items – hair and beauty bits, craft essentials, jewellery, herbs and spices. If using it near water, I recommend using a water-based varnish to seal it.

YOU WILL NEED

A wooden box with drawers
Paint suitable for wood – I used
    Laura Ashley eggshell paint in
    Pale Eau de Nil
Paintbrush
Fine or medium grade sandpaper
Clear matt varnish
Metal label holders in an antique
    finish
Screws and screwdriver
Brown paper
Calligraphy pen (optional)

STEP 1 - PAINT BOX

Give your box two coats of furniture paint, allowing the first coat to dry thoroughly before applying the second. If you plan to use this for food or drink items I suggest you don't paint the inside, or choose a paint that can be safely used on food preparation surfaces.

STEP 2 - SAND

If you'd like your box to have a distressed look, once it is dry, give the edges and corners a rub with fine or medium sandpaper to reveal some of the wood underneath.

STEP 3 - VARNISH

Give it a good brush down, then give the box a coat of clear matt varnish, allow it to dry and repeat. Let dry.

STEP 4 - ATTACH LABEL HOLDERS

Decide where you'd like to place your metal holders. Once they're all aligned mark the screw holes with a pencil – this will ensure they don't end up wonky. Screw them all in place. *See pictures: middle and bottom.*

STEP 5 - ADD LABELS

Finally, add your labels. I used old brown paper and wrote my labels using a calligraphy pen, but you could just as easily print some out, or cut out the names from your existing tea cartons. Pop in your tea, put the kettle on and enjoy a well-earned brew. *See picture: opposite.*

SEASONAL WREATH MAKING

Beautiful wreaths can be very expensive to buy, yet making wreaths is incredibly easy. It's well worth having a go at this, because once you've made your first one, you'll get such a kick out of your creation and you'll have the confidence to do it year after year, for any occasion. We have wreaths that come out for every season now. I've made a faux Christmas wreath that I add fresh holly and foliage to each year. I have a faux moss wreath with rustic twigs and pretty little eggs to hang at Easter. I've made dried lavender wreaths in the summer and I always make a fresh autumn wreath too.

I'll show you how to make two very simple autumn wreaths and, of course, the same principles can be adapted to any theme or season.

TIPS FOR WREATH MAKING

I always like my wreath designs to look very natural and a little wild, regardless of the season. Here are a few things to bear in mind for an even, balanced wreath.

KEEP TO A PATTERN. Regardless of the style of wreath you're making, if making a circular wreath, stick to a pattern. My pattern for the wreath opposite was pine cone/leaves/seedhead/twigs, and then repeat. You can add other random elements, such as the feathers and delicate grasses, at the end.

RULE OF THREE. When it comes to floral arrangements, bouquets and wreaths, many florists like to work in odd numbers as this looks more aesthetically pleasing. It matters less with a wreath like my autumn leaves wreath as it all blends together so well. But if you're making a wreath with more distinctive blooms, the rule of three is worth remembering.

THE SAME DIRECTION. When placing your components on the wreath, face them all in the same direction. They can still be at different angles, as long as they're facing the same way. Then work backwards so the next piece lays on top of the last piece, thus hiding its stem and join.

PROJECT

FAUX AUTUMN LEAVES WREATH

This will take no more than 10 minutes to make. I wanted to show you just how easy it is to make a wreath using an artificial garland. Faux foliage isn't for everyone; in fact, I used to be a bit of a snob when it came to artificial flowers. However, there is definitely a place for it, especially when used alongside real foliage. Faux garlands are ideal as a base to which you simply add fresh foliage each year. When the season is over, remove the fresh foliage and pack the wreath away until next year. You could also add weatherproof battery-powered fairy lights to this – perfect for Christmas.

YOU WILL NEED

Rattan, vine or willow wreath base
Floral wire
Wire cutters
Faux autumn leaves garland
Glue gun
Pine cones
Feathers
String (optional)

STEP 1 - ATTACH FAUX GARLAND

Cut a small piece of floral wire and bind the end of the garland to the back of the wreath. (Note: using a glue gun to secure the garland may melt the plastic.)

STEP 2 - WRAP GARLAND

Now wrap the garland around the wreath, and keep wrapping it all the way around until it meets the other end. Now either snip it or take it around a second time. Then secure the end with floral wire.

STEP 3 - ADD FRESH MATERIAL

Finally, using the glue gun, add any embellishments such as pine cones, twigs and feathers at regular intervals. Hang with string and enjoy!

PROJECT

REAL AUTUMN WREATH

Autumn, oh how I love thee! We bask in your warm milky light, kicking our heels through your luminous gold leaves (risky, but worth it)! Cosy in our chunky knits, we sip a spiced apple cider and huddle around a crackling fire. I can think of no better way to celebrate autumn in all her glory than to hang a beautiful wreath covered in her spoils.

YOU WILL NEED

Selection of dried leaves, dried flower heads, twigs, pine cones and feathers
Secateurs/pruning shears (or scissors that can cut through stalks and twigs)
Rattan, vine or willow wreath base
Glue gun
String (optional)

STEP 1 - PREPARE DRIED MATERIAL

Put your dried goods into separate piles and cut off any long stems. If you're planning to hang the wreath with string, tie a length to the wreath base now.

STEP 2 - DECORATE

Plug in the glue gun. When it's hot enough, dollop a good blob of glue on the wreath. Pick up a pine cone and hold it in place on the glue for five seconds, or until it stays in place. It's as simple as that.

STEP 3 - FILL WREATH BASE

Now continue all the way around, referring to the wreath-making tips on page 236. Enjoy playing with the positioning of each piece – some might want to be angled up, or angled down, more to one side, more to the centre, and so on. Then keep going until you are back at the start. When finished, you can embellish it further with feathers and delicate grasses. Hang and enjoy your handiwork.

THE CHILDREN'S ROOM

IF THERE IS A ROOM IN THE HOUSE
WHERE YOU CAN REALLY ALLOW YOUR CREATIVITY
TO RUN WILD, IT'S THE CHILDREN'S ROOM

Children's rooms can be a true blank canvas in your home, where you can let your own inner child take over with the decorating a little! Our offspring are only little for a short space of time, so creating a magical environment where they can grow and thrive and that will capture their imagination will be a gift for both of you. If you're anything like me, you'll get more satisfaction from making things for this room (and for them) than for any other part of the house.

INTRODUCING COLOUR

Children love colour, and it plays such a crucial part in their development. While our love for muted pastel tones might have been acceptable to our babies and toddlers, as soon as our kids are walking and talking those sage linen dungarees that we have been crowbarring them into will be tossed aside in favour of sparkly bright rainbow tutus and Marvel costumes. It is inevitable and healthy that there should come a time when our influence over their style and environment plays second fiddle to theirs, but I think it can work both ways. My little girl's love of colour has definitely rubbed off on me and has encouraged me to bring more colour into our lives, and to recognise the lack of it in certain areas. However, I do think there is a way we can fill their rooms with colour, fun and vibrancy without it being overbearing to the adults of the house.

CHOOSING A THEME

When it comes to decorating a child's room, I suggest avoiding an overall theme. If you go out and buy Paw Patrol curtains, light fittings, rugs and wallpaper, the chances are by next month your child will have moved on to something else. You'll either need to redecorate, or for the foreseeable future they'll be stuck with an environment they're not enjoying or benefiting from. It's a much safer bet to keep the big-ticket items neutral with a plain colour or a simple pattern, so that you can introduce more

colours, images and characters through pictures, removable wall stickers, bunting, light shades and cushions, in other words the accessories that can easily be changed and updated.

I like to feature as many different themes and characters in my daughter Frankie's room as I can, so there are multiple worlds and rich images to capture her imagination. A lot of the decor is inspired by nature – I've no doubt there will come a time when she'll try to strong-arm me into covering her entire room with Peppa Pig, but for now she seems content with the mix of flower fairies, felted flowers, woodland creatures, flower garlands, fairy lights, bunting, snow globes, artworks from classic stories such as *The Wind in the Willows* and Brambly Hedge, and Pooh Bear wall stickers. By avoiding a single theme you can keep the room fun, varied and easily adaptable to your child's changing interests.

There were so many ideas I could have shared in this chapter but there simply wasn't room for all of them, so here are just a few of mine and Frankie's favourite projects. All of these can be adapted to your own style. Also, do take a look at the children's lampshade project on page 177.

PROJECT

PAINTED STENCILLED CHEST OF DRAWERS

When I asked Frankie what colour we should paint the secondhand chest of drawers I bought for her room, she replied 'pink' without hesitation. I wasn't keen on bringing hot fuchsia pink into her pretty little bedroom, so I looked around at various shades of pink and quickly fell in love with Annie Sloan's Scandinavian Pink chalk paint. Luckily Frankie approved of my choice!

Initially I planned to decoupage paper onto the drawer fronts, but when I saw Annie's stencil selection I decided on a different approach. I used a two-tone colour technique for this project by using chalk paint in Old White as a base, applying the Scandinavian Pink on top, and then stencilling on top using Old White. Distressing the drawers at the end of this process allowed some of the white to peek through. If you want to save time and use just one colour for the drawers and another for the stencil, that would be absolutely fine too.

Don't be too regimented when stencilling. You can turn the stencil on its side and upside down to get some variations. You can even use just one part of the stencil. Above all, have fun with it and you'll get a beautiful design. If it does go wrong at any point, don't panic. Keep going, then once dry you can always go back over any mistakes with the pink paint, then re-stencil.

I love to use furniture wax on chalk paint as it gives such a beautiful finish, but as this piece would be living in Frankie's room it needed to be hard-wearing so I opted to finish it with a clear matt lacquer instead. This is a very simple but effective upcycling project but be warned – you may want to go and stencil everything you own afterwards!

YOU WILL NEED

Chest of drawers

Low-tack masking tape

Furniture chalk paint – I used Annie Sloan
Chalk Paint in Old White and
Scandinavian Pink

Paint brush – I used the Annie Sloan round
brush for chalk paint

Fine or medium grade sandpaper, for
distressing

Furniture stencil – I used the Annie Sloan
Mexican Birds stencil

Clear furniture wax, clear furniture lacquer
or matt varnish

Wax brushes or lint-free cloth

*Tip: Consider doing a patch test first to avoid tannins
seeping through and yellowing your lovely white paint,
even if your base colour is dark (see page 97).*

STEP 1 - PREPARE

With chalk paint there is no need to sand or
prime. Mask off any areas you don't want to
paint – I applied tape around the edges of
the drawers. I unscrewed the handles so
they were loose but still attached, in order
to paint on and around them easily. *See
picture: top.*

STEP 2 - APPLY FIRST COAT

Stir the Old White paint and apply straight
to the drawers. It may help to turn the
drawers upside down so that you can
begin painting the bottom first. Rather
than making long, sweeping brush strokes
(which will show the brush lines more),
instead move the brush back and forth in
every direction as you paint until the piece
is covered. This technique is much quicker

and you will get a lovely, smooth and rustic-looking finish. Allow to dry. Then flip and finish the top of the drawers. Allow to dry. *See picture: opposite middle.*

STEP 3 - APPLY SECOND COLOUR

Now repeat step 2, this time using one or two coats of the Scandinavian Pink. I applied two coats but if you'd like it to look more patchy or faded, one coat would suffice. The great thing about chalk paint is that you can play with it. You can water it down to create more of a wash effect, and if you do try something and don't like it, just let it dry and go over it again. *See picture: opposite bottom.*

STEP 4 - DISTRESS

You can distress after stencilling or before (I chose to do it before). I didn't want to take too much paint off when distressing so I used a medium to fine sandpaper. I focused on taking a little paint off along the edges, the corners and from the centre and edges of the drawer handles too. When finished, give it a light brush down with a soft brush to remove any sanding dust.

STEP 5 - STENCIL

Now for the fun bit! Tape your stencil to the furniture with masking tape. Dip your brush in the Old White paint, remove the excess and begin painting onto the gaps in the stencil. I find a light stabbing technique is more effective than brushing the paint on. The key to good stencilling is to avoid overloading the brush as that can lead to unwanted splodges. When using a stencil repeatedly, wipe excess paint from the stencil occasionally. If you do get the odd mark on the piece, I wouldn't worry too much, as it's unlikely to be noticed with a pattern like this and it can be fixed later. Once finished, carefully lift the stencil off, wipe if necessary, then reapply to the next area and continue until you have covered all the intended areas. Allow to dry. *See picture: below.*

STEP 6 - APPLY WAX OR LACQUER

When the paint is completely dry, finish with one or two coats of furniture wax, varnish or lacquer. I used lacquer for this project, which you can apply in the same manner as the paint. Once you've got an area covered you can also do some light feathering over it. This is when you sweep the paint or lacquer lightly with only the tip of the brush. This reduces brush marks and can be done in one direction or every direction. When dry, remove the masking tape and re-affix the handles.

PROJECT

DECOUPAGED CHILDREN'S FURNITURE

When it comes to characterful children's furniture, I find there is a limited variety available in the shops and online, unless you are willing to spend a lot of money, and considering they're going to grow out of it in a few years, this probably isn't worth the investment. For Frankie's second birthday her grandparents asked what she might like, and I suggested a plain, children's table and chairs set from Ikea as it was reasonably priced and relatively well made. Her grandparents were quite surprised by my choice (they know I usually like my furniture to look like it's fallen out of a fairy glen!) but if you can't find what you're looking for, the best thing is to create it yourself. That, in a nutshell, is how I became a crafter after all. So here is a simple, straightforward decoupage project that anyone can do.

This is a great project to do with kids, especially if they're a bit older.

You can use any kind of paper for this project, such as magazines, comics, picture books or napkins. For this project I used an old faded novel, some torn up vintage floral paper and some images I found in secondhand children's books. See pages 37–49 for detailed decoupage instructions.

YOU WILL NEED

Table and chairs
PVA or Mod Podge glue – I used PVA
Decorative papers of your choice

Paintbrush
Clear gloss varnish (optional)
Clear matt varnish

STEP 1 - DILUTE GLUE

Pour your glue into a container and add a splash of water until it has a thinner consistency. This will make it easier to apply and reduce bubbling.

STEP 2 - TEAR PAPERS

Tear your paper up into pieces. Anything goes sizewise, although bear in mind the smaller you make them the longer it will take. If you're using a few different types of images, I suggest keeping them in separate piles so you can alternate between them.

STEP 3 - APPLY GLUE

Apply a thin layer of glue to one area (thick layers lead to bubbling), then place a piece of paper on the glue and put a thin layer of glue on top of the paper. Then slowly work your way over the rest of the piece. My method was to cover an area with just the text papers, then apply the florals, and finally add the pictures on the top, or you could alternate as you go. Continue until the surface is covered and allow it to dry completely. *See picture: middle.*

STEP 4 - VARNISH

Apply two coats of varnish. I gave mine a coat of clear gloss first (which dries crystal clear), then once dry I followed it with a coat of clear matt varnish so it was waterproof, durable and had a matt finish (two coats of matt can sometimes look a little milky). *See pictures: bottom and opposite.*

PROJECT

SWEET AND SIMPLE BUNTING

To celebrate the coming of spring and all things bright and beautiful,
I decided to make some bunting for Frankie's room. This is the easiest
bunting you can make – you don't need advanced skills and it will take less
than an hour. I used a simple running stitch, but you can just as easily use
fabric glue. I like two or three contrasting fabrics but really, anything goes.

YOU WILL NEED

Cardboard and pen, for the template
Scissors
Cotton fabric
Fabric scissors
Brown string
Brown thread and needle, or fabric
    glue

STEP 1 - CUT OUT FABRIC

On a piece of cardboard draw a
triangle the size of the bunting you
want. Cut it out to form a template.
Use the template to draw six triangles
(or as many as you like) on your
fabric, then cut them out. *See picture:
opposite bottom left.*

STEP 2 - ARRANGE FABRIC PIECES

Place the fabric pieces right side up on
a table at regular intervals. Then lay
the string along the top so you can see
how much string you need to cut
(allow enough to make hanging hoops).

STEP 3 - ATTACH TO STRING

- To use fabric glue, apply a thin
line of glue along the top edge of
the bunting and lay the long piece of
string along the top, one triangle at
a time. Leave to dry.
- To sew, lay your long piece of string
along the top edge of the bunting and
pin in place. Thread your needle with
a long piece of brown thread and tie
a knot in the end. Sew each piece of
fabric to the string using an in-and-out
running stitch (see page 30). To make
sure it was secure I made an extra
vertical stitch in between. After the
last stitch at the end of each triangle,
tie a knot to finish it off and cut the
thread. *See picture: opposite bottom right.*

STEP 4 - FINISH OFF

Tie a small loop at each end of the
string and your bunting is now ready
to hang.

PROJECT

COUNTRY COTTAGE BIRDHOUSE

I really enjoyed making this project and while it was initially to house my string and ribbons (as this is not suitable for use outdoors), it is now a lovely addition to Frankie's room. You could use these techniques to decorate the front of a doll's house, too. It may look incredibly intricate, but it really isn't. It's a lot of fun to do and aside from the supplies, all you need is glue and a bit of patience.

YOU WILL NEED

A wooden birdhouse
Glue – I used PVA glue, but would
   recommend using a stronger, fast-
   drying glue to save time
Decorative gravel in cream and green
Selection of faux feathers – I used
   3 packets
Selection of paper roses in green and
   peach
Bunch of faux daisies
Bunch of tiny faux rosebuds
Wired pip berries in green
Thin circular stick (such as a knitting
   needle)
Sticky tape

STEP 1 - ADD CREAM GRAVEL

Cover one side of the birdhouse in an even layer of glue, and sprinkle with an even layer of the cream gravel. Allow to dry (I used PVA glue, but this took quite a while to dry which is why I'd recommend a quick-drying glue if possible). Once dry, repeat on the next side until all four sides are covered.

STEP 2 - ADD GREEN GRAVEL

Then apply another layer of glue to just the lower half of the cream gravel sides and sprinkle with green gravel to represent 'ivy'. Allow to dry. *See picture: top.*

STEP 3 - DECORATE ROOF

Starting from the lower edges of the roof, dab some glue onto the wood and place the feathers at evenly spaced intervals. Then do another row (in between the previous ones) and work your way towards the top. Keep the small feathers for the top and edges of the roof. *See picture: middle.*

STEP 4 - PREPARE FLOWERS

Split the flowers into smaller bunches and mix and match as you like, then use one stem to bind each bunch. Wind the wires around a thin circular stick (such as a thin knitting needle) a few times. Then slide the bunch off and bend the bottom up so it can stand. Then put it to one side ready to glue. Next twist together two strands of wired berries and wrap with the occasional flower – this is going to 'grow up' the front of the birdhouse. *See pictures: opposite bottom and here top and middle.*

STEP 5 - ATTACH FLOWERS

Now it's time to start gluing the flowers in place. Start with the bigger pieces first (like the strands of berries) and allow them to dry. Don't be afraid to cheat – for example, I taped the top of the entwined berries to the roof in order to hold them in place. Working your way along, start to add more flowers. When all the bunches have been glued into place, you can use some of the leftover flower heads to fill in gaps along the bottom. *See picture: bottom.*

PROJECT

DOLL'S HOUSE MAKEOVER

When shopping around for a doll's house for Frankie, I was really shocked by the price of them. I had my heart set on a pretty wooden painted one that would last a long time. I love the sentiment of handmade things being passed down, so this doll's house was a real joy to customise.

I found this house on eBay. If you have any leftover furniture chalk paint, do use that. However, all I had at the time were some Farrow & Ball emulsion sample pots (usually for painting walls, not wood), so that is what I used here. I've used emulsion on little projects before and providing the wood is porous and you follow with a couple of coats of varnish, it is absolutely fine.

For the inside I had some decoupage paper books so used these as wallpaper, or you could simply paint the walls. I finished it off by adding two sets of copper wire fairy lights to illuminate the rooms. You needn't add real flowers to the front if you don't have them – perhaps you could try floral stickers, or add flowers like the ones in the birdhouse on page 257.

YOU WILL NEED

Wooden doll's house

Wooden doll's house furniture (optional)

Selection of paper for wallpaper

Scrap paper

Scissors (or rotary cutter and cutting mat)

PVA glue

Lint-free cloth

Sample pots or leftover paint – I used Farrow & Ball in All White (front and sides of house), Brassica (front door), Bone (windows) and Arsenic (roof)

Polyvine Clear Acrylic Decorator's Varnish in dead flat, or clear matt water-based varnish

Selection of thin artists' paintbrushes.

Pressed flowers (optional, see page 222)

String of battery-operated copper wire fairy lights (optional)

Sticky tape (optional)

STEP 1 - CUT WALLPAPER

Cut all the papers to be used on the inside walls to the right size using scissors or a rotary cutter and cutting mat. I used scrap paper initially to get the right size, so I could mess around with it, fold it and crease it until I had the right size. Then I used it as a template to cut out the pieces from the 'good stuff'.

STEP 2 - PAPER AND VARNISH INTERIOR

Once the wallpapers are cut out, lay the doll's house flat and starting from the top, begin to apply. Starting from one corner, apply a thin layer of watered-down PVA glue directly onto the wall, lay the first piece on, and smooth the paper out with a clean, dry cloth from the centre outwards, removing any bubbles by pushing them towards the edge. Work your way along each wall, wiping away any excess glue. Do this until the walls on each floor are covered. Leave for 24 hours until completely dry, then give the paper two coats of clear matt varnish.

STEP 3 - PAINT OUTSIDE

You can paint the outside of the house in any order you like. Using a thin brush, I started by painting the windows first, then the brickwork, the front door and the front of the house, finishing with the roof. Give all the paintwork two coats of paint and leave to dry. *See picture: middle.*

STEP 4 - PAINT FURNITURE

While you are painting the front, have all the doll's furniture nearby, so when you finish painting the front door, for example, you can paint a couple of the pieces of furniture in the same colour. Do this with each paint

colour and you'll have a lovely selection of painted furniture.

STEP 5 - ADD PRESSED FLOWERS

If you wish to add pressed flowers, lay the doll's house down flat. Pour some PVA glue into a little pot, but don't dilute it this time. Take a thin paintbrush, apply a decent amount of glue to the brush and carefully apply it along the length of the flower, then lay it in place. If it's a delicate flower and you think it may disintegrate by applying glue to it, apply the glue directly to the doll's house, then lay the flower on top of the glue. I recommend using delicate flowers for this, as chunky flowers don't press or stick well. Once finished, leave to dry. *See pictures: opposite bottom, and here top and bottom.*

STEP 6 - VARNISH

Once the flowers are dry, keep the house laid flat and give just the front and the sides a coat of varnish. Leave to dry and repeat once or even twice more. It's better to give it two or three thin coats of varnish than one or two thick coats, in order to avoid drips. After each coat, open up the house to check you are not dripping through, leave to dry, then stand the house up and repeat on the roof and the back. Also give all your painted doll's house furniture a couple of coats of varnish too.

STEP 7 - ADD LIGHTS

Once dry you can add some battery operated fairy lights if you wish. I fixed the switch to the back of the doll's house, then I ran the wire around the edges of every ceiling and secured using a little bit of sticky tape (you could use glue but the tape doesn't show one bit).

THE CHILDREN'S ROOM

STOCKISTS

Annie Sloan
anniesloan.com
Chalk paints, stencils, brushes.
Paint used in Frottage Painted
Chairs (page 193), Painted
Stencilled Chest of Drawers
(page 247)

Brian Seymour artist
blsartist.com
Artwork featured on page 112

Briwax
briwax.com
Briwax used in painting and
waxing basic techniques on
pages 55–59, Distressed Bedside
Table (page 197), Old Writing
Desk Makeover (page 201),
Wallpapered Corner Cabinet
(page 205)

Calendars
calendarclub.co.uk
Calendars used in Decoupage
Bathroom Wall (page 103)

Farrow & Ball
farrow-ball.com
Farrow & Ball paint used in
Painted Doors (page 191),
creating spaces (page 90, 97, 98,
101), Doll's House Makeover
(page 261)

Flower Fairy treasury book
wob.com
Images used in standard
decoupage (page 43)

Hops garland
essentiallyhops.co.uk
Featured in framing with hops
(page 101)

Just Fabrics
justfabrics.co.uk
Laura Ashley fabric used in
Ribbon-Tie Curtains (page 143),
Voyage fabric used in Fabric
Lampshade (page 167)

Lampshade kits
dannells.com
Used in all lampshade projects
(pages 167–177)

Laura Ashley
diy.com
Laura Ashley furniture
paint used in Old Writing
Desk Makeover (page 201),
Wallpapered Corner Cabinet
(page 205), Tea Storage Caddy
(page 233)
Laura Ashley wallpaper used
in Old Writing Desk Makeover
(page 201), Wallpapered Corner
Cabinet (page 205)

Mod Podge
modpodge.co.uk
Glue in matt finish used in
projects throughout the book

Marie Kondo
konmari.com
*The life-Changing Magic of
Tidying* (page 72)

Rust-Oleum furniture paint
rustoleumcolours.co.uk
Chalk paint used in Distressed
Bedside Table (page 197),
Floral Farmhouse Welsh Dresser
(page 209)

Spoonflower
spoonflower.com
Fabric used in No-Sew Tassel
Cushion (page 127), Simple
Cushion (page 131), Keyhole
Cover Hanger (page 159)

Wild Paper
wildpaper.co.uk
Natural handmade Lokta
tissue paper used in Pressed
Wildflower Lampshade
(page 173)

Wreath
www.gardentrading.co.uk
Wreath used in Nature
Chandelier (page 179)

INDEX

ACKNOWLEDGEMENTS

Writing this book has been a true labour of love, but it would not have been at all possible without the help, guidance, and support of the following people.

TO MY FAMILY

Firstly I would like to say a deeply heartfelt thank you to Andy, my incredible husband and photographer – your skill, patience, humour and cooking skills have kept me going throughout our marriage, as well as through this book. To my darling girl Frankie, my little ray of sunshine – you are my favourite crafting companion. To my little dog Ralphy – you've been there from the very beginning old boy; thanks for opening my eyes to the natural world all those years ago. To my folks Del and Val – your love and belief in me have always been a constant; you have made my life a happy one. To my wonderful in-laws David and Coring – thank you for always being there; I truly lucked out landing you as MIL and DIL. To all of my family, especially my mum, niece Kayleigh, Liz and my brother Jaylee for rallying around me armed with paintbrushes at the drop of a hat. To Brian Seymour (my uncle Titch) for his beautiful artwork. Finally, thank you to Rita and Jack – I miss you dearly, I may never have discovered my love for craft had it not been for you.

TO MY FRIENDS

Thank you to my cottage crafters for all you've taught me and for always being there to pick me up when I dropped a stitch. To Ros, for being there with me at the beginning; I so wish you were here at the end. To my sewing guru Trish for your expertise and friendship – I'm grateful to this book for bringing us together. To lovely Joe for your knowledge in all things DIY. To Eva Katzler for your wisdom when I need it most. To Tina Sales for your help, friendship and beautiful artwork. To Penny Perret for your enthusiasm and inspiration. To Suzy for being there for me and Frankie at the drop of a hat. To Sarah and Emily for your thoughtfulness and doorstep 'care packages' and finally to my soul sisters Mim and Michelle – thank you for being my everything.

TO OTHER CONTRIBUTORS

Thank you to Farrow & Ball and Annie Sloan for your help and support.

TO MY AMAZING TEAM

A very big thank you to Murdoch Books and my publisher Céline Hughes for giving me this wonderful opportunity, and for being so supportive throughout. A big thank also to my dream team for your guidance, patience and help in bringing this book to life. I'm extremely grateful to Patrick Budge, my brilliant book designer and the Giles to my Buffy; to Gillian Haslam, my forever-patient copy-editor; and to my friend and manager Carly Martin-Gammon, without whom this book would never have found its way into the universe.

AND FINALLY TO MY READERS

Thank you for joining me on this journey; it means the world. I hope you enjoy making your way through these pages as much as I've enjoyed writing them for you.

Published in 2024 by Murdoch Books, an imprint
of Allen & Unwin

Murdoch Books UK
Ormond House
26–27 Boswell Street
London WC1N 3JZ
Phone: +44 (0) 20 8785 5995
murdochbooks.co.uk
info@murdochbooks.co.uk

Murdoch Books Australia
Cammeraygal Country
83 Alexander Street
Crows Nest NSW 2065
Phone: +61 (0)2 8425 0100
murdochbooks.com.au
info@murdochbooks.com.au

For corporate orders and custom publishing,
contact our business development team at
salesenquiries@murdochbooks.com.au

Publisher: Céline Hughes
Editor: Gillian Haslam
Designer: Patrick Budge
Photographer: Andy Platts
Production Director, UK: Niccolò De Bianchi
Production Director, Australia: Lou Playfair

Murdoch Books Australia acknowledges the
Traditional Owners of the Country on which
we live and work. We pay our respects to all
Aboriginal and Torres Strait Islander Elders, past
and present.

ISBN 978 1 922616784

 A catalogue record for this
book is available from the
National Library of Australia

A catalogue record for this book is available from
the British Library.

Colour reproduction by Born Group, London, UK

Printed by 1010 Printing International Limited,
China

10 9 8 7 6 5 4 3 2 1